European Agency for Safety and Health at Work

Occupational safety
and health
in marketing and
procurement

SYSTEMS AND PROGRAMMES

A great deal of additional information on the European Union is available on the Internet.
It can be accessed through the Europa server (http://europa.eu.int).

Cataloguing data can be found at the end of this publication.

Luxembourg: Office for Official Publications of the European Communities, 2000

ISBN 92-95007-01-8

© European Agency for Safety and Health at Work, 2000
Reproduction is authorised provided the source is acknowledged.

Printed in Belgium

European Agency for Safety and Health at Work

Contents

FOREWORD	5
SUMMARY	7
1. INTRODUCTION	11
2. OSH IN MARKETING AT COMPANY LEVEL	17
2.1. Marketing by bus operators — Social accounting by Linjebus	18
2.2. Marketing of ergonomic hand tools — Fiskars	24
2.3. Marketing of office equipment — König + Neurath	33
2.4. Marketing of car cleaning products — Polytop Autopflege	39
2.5. Marketing in employment service sector — Vedior BIS	44
3. OSH IN GENERIC MARKETING SYSTEMS	49
3.1. Marketing of building products — Indoor climate labelling scheme	50
3.2. Marketing office equipment — The TCO labelling scheme	57
3.3. Marketing management systems — The 6E management scheme	62
3.4. Marketing of bakery equipment — NF HSA by Bongard	68
4. GOVERNMENTAL MARKETING INITIATIVES	73
4.1. Stimulating OSH marketing — The Danish working environment label	74
5. OSH IN PROCUREMENT AT COMPANY LEVEL	81
5.1. Procurement in the construction sector — the Danish landworks, Øresund fixed link	82
5.2. Procurement in an industrial plant — Renault Technocenter	89
5.3. Procurement in the electricity sector — Electrabel	94
5.4. Procurement in the pharmaceutical industry — AstraZeneca management concept	100
6. OSH IN GENERIC PROCUREMENT SYSTEMS	107
6.1. Procurement of cleaning agents — IKA	108
6.2. Stimulating OSH procurement — BeschaffungsService Austria	112
6.3. Stimulating OSH procurement — VCA checklist	118
6.4. Stimulating OSH procurement — The safety passport scheme	128
6.5. Stimulating OSH procurement — Biganos EIG	135
6.6. Ethical investment — Triodos Bank	140

7. GOVERNMENTAL PROCUREMENT INITIATIVES 147
   7.1. Stimulating OSH procurement — The good neighbour scheme: HSE 148
   7.2. Belgian policy regarding OSH in procurement 153

8. CONCLUSIONS 161
   8.1. Marketing 162
   8.2. Procurement 163
   8.3. Scale of application 165

Appendices

APPENDIX 1: METHODOLOGY AND DATA COLLECTION 169

APPENDIX 2: ACKNOWLEDGEMENTS 171

European Agency for Safety and Health at Work

FOREWORD

According to Regulation 2063/94 of 18 July 1994 article 3.1h, the Agency shall provide technical, scientific and economic information on methods and tools for implementing preventive activities. The Administrative Board of the Agency consequently decided to include a study on new ways to improve occupational safety and health (OSH) in the Agency's Work Programmes 1999 and 2000. The topic of the study was OSH as a specific subject for subcontracting (procurement) and marketing.

The 22 case examples from 9 Member States presented here provide detailed information of the systems used and also include opinions of key stakeholders such as representatives of the developers of the schemes, company management, safety and health managers, purchasers, customers, and worker representatives. The study does not seek to promote any of the particular schemes presented. The aim is to increase awareness and exchange experience on the issue by providing a catalogue of possible schemes as well as to stimulate discussion on the possible use of these relative new instruments.

The Agency would like to thank Sonja Hagen Mikkelsen and Marchen Vinding Petersen from COWI consultants and all other organisations who participated in this study. In particular we would like to thank all those companies willing to share their experiences. Without their contributions the project could not have been completed. Finally, the Agency would like to thank the members of its Thematic Network Group Systems and Programmes for their valuable comments and suggestions with respect to the project.

The European Agency for Safety and Health at Work

November 2000

SUMMARY

This catalogue includes 22 case studies, which primarily illustrates voluntary initiatives taken by companies or governments in order to:

- market their products, goods and services and declare that their products/services are safe to be used in a work situation or produced under good internal working conditions.
- select subcontractors/suppliers on the basis of their safety and health performances;

The companies are located within the Member States of the European Union and represent smaller as well as larger companies within various sectors. The initiatives are based on different approaches and instruments, developed by the companies themselves, independent institutions or national authorities. The schemes represented include one or more of the following elements:

- tender criteria;
- management systems;
- certifications;
- labels;
- declarations;
- general communication;
- accounts.

The described initiatives are not selected to be representative for all existing schemes on the European scene, but should together represent initiatives, which may inspire other companies and organisations, either to adopt the schemes or to make the necessary modifications to adapt the schemes to their specific sector and needs.

The description of each case study aims to provide an objective description of the practices, the purpose and function of the practice and an assessment of where similar initiatives seems applicable and effective. The assessment is based on a number of interviews with key respondents. In general the parties which have developed the specific scheme, the company using the scheme and suppliers/customers of the products and services delivered by the company are interviewed.

This study describes a number of schemes representing how occupational safety and health (OSH) can be targeted through six different approaches:
- marketing at company level;
- generic marketing systems;
- governmental marketing initiatives.
- procurement at company level;
- generic procurement systems;
- governmental procurement initiatives;

The economic aspects of the different schemes have not been evaluated as part of the project. There is however, no doubt that for the companies involved the economic benefits on the bottom line are key motivators, whether it be a result of a reduction in lost time accidents, higher productivity or increased market shares.

In many countries the social partners have become increasingly involved in voluntary schemes promoting safety and health in the workplace either by supporting the schemes once they are implemented or through direct partnership and participation in the schemes.

Marketing at company level

Just as many companies have developed their own individual schemes for procurement, the same is the situation in relation to marketing of products and services. These marketing schemes reflect the needs and priorities of the customers and the market in general. As the focus on OSH performance and qualities of products and services is increasing, there is also an increasing demand for measuring, documenting and communicating these qualities in the marketing material and to assist the customers in order to use the products and services in a safe and healthy manner.

A new trend is the introduction of social and ethical aspects in the evaluation of the working environment. One example of social accounting is presented in this report. The theme is quite new when applied in an OSH context, and the experiences are therefore limited. It must however be expected that this concept may gain ground in the future and increase the focus on quality of life in the working environment.

Generic marketing systems

Certification schemes and labels based on environmental performance have become more common as marketing tools over the last few decades. OSH criteria have been included to varying degrees and schemes focusing primarily on OSH and secondly on the environment have been launched.

Among the generic marketing systems described in the catalogue are labelling schemes for products and equipment and certification of management systems and subcontractors based on OSH criteria.

Certification of contractors and management systems in the service sector in relation to OSH, has become a more strong marketing tool as it is also often a demand from the client companies in the purchasing situation. These schemes therefore go hand in hand.

Governmental marketing system

One marketing scheme initiated at governmental level is described. This scheme, which aims at certifying companies with a good OSH performance, is still in the development stage. One of the goals is to attract employees and another to establish a competitive advantage in the market. It is a so-called soft economic and management incentive for improving OSH performance beyond what is required by the legislation.

Procurement at company level

Many companies and organisations have developed their own individual procurement schemes reflecting their requirement to the products, goods and services they purchase.

The motivation to develop, adopt or join a specific scheme can vary among companies and sectors. In some high risk sectors like the construction industry the obvious risks and high accident rates and thereby the related costs and risks of delays have been key drivers in the development of some of the presented schemes. In example the case study illustrating experiences gained from building the landworks of the Øresund link (linking Denmark and Sweden). The goal for the building owner was to reduce the number of occupational accidents by 50 % compared to the average within the building industry. The strategy to obtain the goal included OSH and environmental requirements when inviting tenders; establishing an organisation to follow up and carry out auditing and initiation of a campaign communicating to all stakeholders that 'any accident is one too many'.

Some of the schemes originally developed within the construction industry are adopted and adjusted to the needs in other sectors, as it has also been the case for some of the schemes presented in the catalogue. And the presented procurement schemes can in principle be applied in every sector with a large demand for contract work and an identified need for good OSH performance.

The tendency over the recent years has been to focus on the training needs for workers and supervisors and to define specific requirements for the contractors' OSH performance, requirements, which are thoroughly monitored and evaluated by the client company or an independent auditor.

According to client companies involved in this study, this approach has proven to be successful and in general resulted in a decrease in accident rates, a growing safety and health awareness, better risk management, better confidence in purchased goods, reduced costs and as an extra benefit, sometimes also cultural changes with respect to OSH within the client company.

When clients make demands on their contractors, there seems to be a tendency for the contractors to pass on the same requirements to their suppliers and thereby increase the positive effects throughout the supply chain.

Generic procurement systems

The increased amount of contract work, has supported the development of more generic procurement schemes for contract work. Using uniform requirements for contractor OSH training or OSH management systems allows for a third party to carry the 'certification' or initial approval of the contractors as well the continuous improvement of the scheme.

Two of the presented schemes have been developed in the petrochemical industry and have not only been widely applied within this sector but are now in a phase of developing into other sectors as well. Part of the success seem to be connected with the simplicity and practicality of the schemes and the fact that the client companies have taken part in the development of the schemes and used their experience to define the criteria.

A working group consisting of representatives of public purchasers, suppliers and a supplier association has developed the third scheme presented in this subcategory. The scheme illustrates a guideline prepared for purchasers of cleaning agents. The guidelines assist purchasers in order to ensure that all relevant requirements regarding the delivery of cleaning agents are included when tenders are prepared. The interviewed parties stress that the use of the guidelines stimulates suppliers to develop more environmentally and occupationally safe cleaning agents; save time for purchasers when preparing and evaluating tenders and save time for the suppliers of cleaning agents because they are met with standardised requirements from more purchasers. The presented guidelines for procurement of cleaning agents can in principle be applied when preparing all kinds of tenders and in a long-term perspective stimulate the development of more environmentally and occupationally safe products and services.

Governmental procurement initiatives

Two procurement schemes initiated by the governments are described. The scheme developed in the UK takes into account that there is a wealth of practical experience in managing safety and health, which could be shared with others — neighbouring firms, suppliers, subcontractors or the wider community. This scheme is widely applicable in all sectors and provides a number of benefits to those who join the scheme — the good neighbours. These benefits include better confidence in the business partners due to increased OSH awareness, the scheme adds to the neighbours experience with contract work and enhances their reputation among business partners and in the community.

The other scheme, which originates from Belgium is based on the development of a number of procedures in the field of purchasing. These procedures cover purchasing of work equipment, protective equipment, dangerous substances, working with contractors, employment agency work and OSH in public contracts. The overall purpose is to control OSH risks in Belgian companies. Unlike the other schemes, this scheme is based on compulsory procedures, which however go beyond the requirements defined in the European directives in this area and can act as inspiration for other Member States. This scheme can be applied in all sectors.

1.

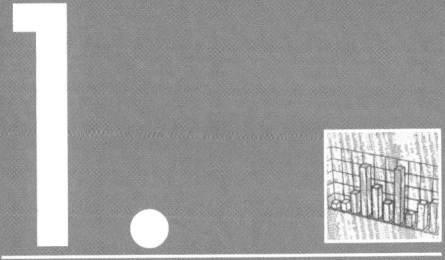

INTRODUCTION

Legislation and enforcement have for many years been the traditional ways of improving the level of occupational safety and health at the workplace in the European Member States. Over the last decades however, governments and sector organisations have increasingly looked into additional ways of promoting safety and health in the workplaces. Also many companies themselves have felt, often independent of regulatory demands, the need to improve occupational safety and health in their production processes, their products and their services. This study describes two of these ways:

- the use of occupational safety and health as a criteria for companies in the purchasing of products and services from other companies;
- the use of occupational safety and health as a marketing element for promoting the sales of their products or services.

Both ways are closely related (see Figure 1).

One should see this development also against the background that companies in general have become more demanding of their suppliers. In their search for quality, firms are also putting increasing emphasis on the safety and health capability of their suppliers, as well as their capacity to deliver the goods. During the past decade companies and public organisations have outsourced an increasing amount of work to contractors and suppliers. They are therefore becoming more dependent on the safety and health performance of their contractors, especially those who are working within their own premises. Consequently they have a fundamental interest in encouraging improvements of the contractors' and suppliers' safety and health performance. Those who do not measure up as either contractors or as subcontractors will find themselves increasingly squeezed out of the supply chain and will have serious problems to survive.

On the other side one can see a tendency for consumers — being either individuals or companies — to become more sensitive to social and ethical values/issues related to the production process. As safety and health characteristics of their production processes, their products and their (accompanying) services have become a more important and distinguishing factor in procurement decisions, many firms use their own efforts to improve safety and health performance as a competitive advantage when marketing products, goods and services.

The dissemination of information and inspiration between companies, sector organisations and even administrations that have been working with these new ways of improving the level of occupational safety and health is crucial for the further development of this approach. Good examples can stimulate firms to raise their own safety and health standard and to put pressure on business partners in the supply chain. Even though the long-term economic benefits can be difficult to measure, many of the improvements are likely to result in increased productivity, competitiveness, and a healthier workforce.

The aim of this study has been to identify and describe interesting examples of how companies in the Member States use occupational safety and health in their marketing and procurement strategies. Either by making demands on the suppliers' safety and health performance or by marketing their goods and

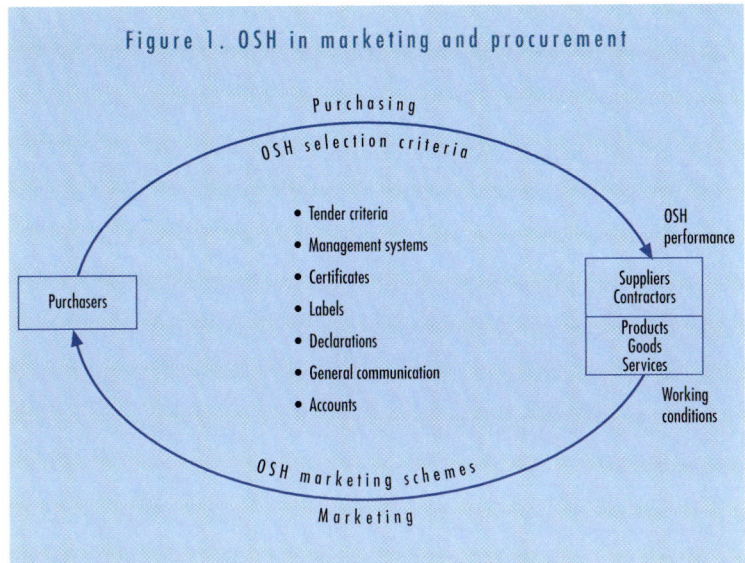

Figure 1. OSH in marketing and procurement

services emphasising company safety and health performance or the safety and health properties of their products as illustrated in Figure 1.

Some initiatives in this area have not been initiated by companies, but by sector-organisation or even with the involvement of national administrations. This can be considered a useful contribution to the development of these new approaches. It is of course efficient to develop these procurement methods jointly at sector level and share experiences. Furthermore it facilitates the access and use of these instruments if they are being taken care of by intermediary organisations.

The examples given in this report have been identified in nine different EU Member States. For each of the levels identified before — that is marketing or procurement at the company, sector or national level — cases are identified and described. The described initiatives (see Table 1.) are not selected to be representative for all existing schemes on the European scene but more to show different ways of promoting safety and health in the workplaces.

This study does not evaluate the economic aspects of the different schemes in use. There is however, no doubt that for the companies involved the economic benefits on the bottom line are key motivators, whether it be a result of a reduction in lost time accidents, higher productivity or increased market shares.

The study is based on interviews with key stakeholders, such as representatives of the developers of the schemes, company management, safety and health managers, purchasers, customers, and worker representatives. Written questionnaires are sometimes used instead of interviews. The methodology and data collection is described in more detail in Appendix 1.

Table 1. Overview of examples of OSH in marketing and procurement

Case company/example	Concept	Sector	Country
Marketing at company level			
Linjebus	Social accounting	Bus (service) company	DK
Fiskars	Documentation of ergonomically friendly design	Manufacturers of hand tools	FIN
König + Neurath	Holistic marketing strategy for office furniture	Manufacturers of office equipment	D
Polytop	Marketing programme and service orientation in a small company	Chemical manufacturer	D
Vedior BIS	Safety awareness: OSH training of temporary workers	Staff agency for temporary workers	F
Generic marketing systems			
Indoor climate label used by Rockfon	Labelling of building materials	Manufacturers of building materials	DK
TCO label	Labelling of office equipment	Manufacturers of computer equipment	S
6E-TCO	Certification of OSH and environmental management systems	Service companies	S
NF HSA label used by Bongard	Labelling of bakery equipment	Manufacturers of bakery equipment	F
Governmental marketing initiatives			
Danish working environment label	Label/certificate based on company OSH performance	Service sector, sectors with difficulties in attracting employees	DK
Procurement at company level			
Øresund fixed link	Tender requirements for contractors, contractor auditing, OSH campaigns	Construction: bridges, tunnels	DK
Renault Technocenter	Tender requirements for contractors, signed safety policy, permanent prevention unit	Construction	F
Electrabel	Requirements for contractors and products	Electricity	B
AstraZeneca	OSH management systems including requirements for contractors	Pharmaceutical	UK
Generic procurement systems			
IKA	Tender requirements for tenderers of cleaning agents	Public purchasing	DK
BeschaffungsService Austria	Procurement guidelines	Public purchasing	A

Case company/example	Concept	Sector	Country
The Dutch VCA system	Safety checklist for contractors	Petrochemical, construction, metal	NL
The passport training scheme, example from Texaco Pembroke plant	Safety passport assigned to contractors passing the passport training	Construction engineering, paper industry	UK
Procurement of contract work through Biganos EIG (econonmic interest grouping) by Smurfit — Cellulose du Pin	Voluntary grouping of subcontracting firms	Industry	F
Triodos Bank	Financial incentive: Ethical investment	Financial	NL
Governmental procurement initiative			
The good neighbour scheme	Client-contractor relationship, sharing expertise in the supply chain	Generally big companies	UK
Procurement policy in Belgium	Compulsory procedures for purchasing products, equipment and services	All sectors	B

2. OSH IN MARKETING AT COMPANY LEVEL

SYSTEMS AND PROGRAMMES

2.1 MARKETING BY BUS OPERATORS — SOCIAL ACCOUNTING BY LINJEBUS

- Denmark
- Internal benchmarking tool
- External marketing tool
- Service companies

2.1.1. Background

This case study describes a voluntary initiative carrying out social accounts for the employees in the Danish division of the bus company Linjebus. Linjebus is one of the largest private bus operators in Denmark. In April 1999 Linjebus published their first social accounts covering the year 1998 and including goals for 1999. The social accounts were one of the first published social accounts in Denmark. The terminology of social accounts may vary between different countries. Social accounts often contain a description of the company's social policies, goals, action plans and obtained results, i.e. within the areas of training, drink policy, easier job and senior policy.

In Denmark, bus operation has been a public task until 1989. From 1989 the public transport authorities have given private or semi-public bus operators the contracts for the work. The contracts can be of varying duration, often 4, 5 or 6 years. When a bus operator is chosen this bus operator is obligated to take over employees who have previously participated in running the bus lines in question. Linjebus has taken over approximately 75 % of their employees. In 1998 Linjebus lost a large contract, which resulted in 400 employees being transferred to the new contract holder. At the same time, Linjebus won other contracts resulting in a take over of another 400 employees. These transfers between different employers affect the employees and it has become more difficult for bus operators to attract and keep bus drivers. In Denmark the bus driver job is considered as a low status job and the physical and psychosocial job conditions are often described as burdensome.

In order to improve the working environment Linjebus has established a number of activities, i.e. training/education, senior policy, securing employees with temporary or lasting reduced working capacity, evaluation of employees' job satisfaction and occupational health and social measures. The goal is to be an attractive workplace, which focuses on social responsibility and the welfare of the employees.

> The purpose of Linjebus' social accounts is to:
> - act as a marketing tool for Linjebus, by being a communication and documentation tool when Linjebus' social performance is discussed with the transport authorities and to provide information to the trade organisations, in order to obtain a reputation as a social responsible company;
> - illustrate Linjebus' performance within social fields, e.g. integration of employees with another ethnic background than Danish;
> - constitute a tool for prioritising and goal-directing Linjebus' future social activities.

2.1.2. Focus on occupational safety and health

Since 1994 Linjebus has sent out questionnaires to all employees asking about job satisfaction. The questionnaire is based on in depth interviews with 40 bus drivers in order to identify which issues they consider being most important regarding their job conditions. The social accounts are basically built on information from these interviews and questionnaires.

Each year a questionnaire is sent out to all employees, bus drivers, workshop employees and salary staff, by an independent consultant. The questionnaire contains 20 questions covering areas such as the transfer between different employers, the daily work and the needs of the individual employee, i.e. issues such as:

- job security;
- corporate spirit;
- work versus leisure time;
- welfare;
- the quality of the buses;
- stress;
- communication between employees and employer representatives;
- qualifications and requirements.

Each question should be answered by giving a score for importance and a score for grade of dissatisfaction. Within each of the three employee groups, the answers are evaluated and goals are set for next year's improvement in the areas given the highest scores. Furthermore, the social accounts present status and goals regarding employee turnover, their age, sex and nationality, seniority, and absence owing to sickness. A third party auditor verifies the compliance of the final social accounts.

2.1.3 Current use of the scheme

As of today, no regulations exist in Denmark for social accounts. The international standard Social Accountability 8000 (SA 8000) is still not used in Denmark. This means that Danish companies choose different ways to carry out their social accounts in order to reflect their specific attitudes, strategies and goals. Therefore, Linjebus' social accounts are also unique. The focus differs from that in SA 8000, which in general pays more attention to ethical questions.

Linjebus carried out their first social account with subsidies from the Danish Ministry of Social Affairs. A Danish consultant company assisted and a certain level of Danish standardisation might be established through knowledge transferred from this consultant.

Linjebus' social accounts include approximately 1 100 employees, 90 % employed as bus drivers and 3 % as workshop employees and 7 % salary staff members. The social accounts are published in Danish and are freely available. In addition the social accounts will be available at Linjebus' home page: www.linjebus.dk. At present, the social accounts are sent to external parties such as the transport authorities, the relevant trade organisations and the Danish Labour Market Training Centre (AMU centre).

2.1.4. Experiences

No third party has evaluated the effect of Linjebus' social accounts.

According to the person responsible for preparing the social accounts in Linjebus, their decision to establish social accounts is primarily based on the following factors. The management in Linjebus assessed that Linjebus had good work conditions. Linjebus had formulated a social policy and had set up specific social goals. The goals were communicated to the employees to make them aware of the on-going work. In order to communicate about status and future goals, the management initiated the social accounts. The social accounts are primarily seen as a management tool to guide the company's internal work and as a tool for marketing the company with regard to the traffic authorities and other external stakeholders, including trade organisations for potential employees. When the yearly questionnaire about job satisfaction is evaluated, the results are discussed with the employees at meetings around the country. Status and future activities are discussed. These meetings, more than the written social accounts are considered to be an important source of information for the employees.

The person responsible for carrying out the social accounts assesses that the social accounts have resulted in a more structured OSH work at Linjebus and has contributed to clarify OSH goals. In contrast to other bus operators in Denmark, Linjebus has no difficulties in attracting employees. One reason might

---

'The social accounts will document the results of implemented social measures, and hereby result in a more focused employee policy, which is based on the employees' need for job satisfaction and improvements.'

Søren Clausen, Adm. Director for Linjebus. 19 April 1999

be the social activities, worker's participation, training/education, etc. in Linjebus.

Linjebus uses their social account to document Linjebus' performance when preparing tenders where the winning part will be the one offering 'best value for money'. Usually, the traffic authorities set up a value assessment model to help themselves decide which proposal offers the best value. The condition for the bus operator's employees and the quality of the buses might be part of these parameters. However, it is difficult to assess whether Linjebus has gained market shares as a direct effect of the social accounts. None of Linjebus' competitors have social accounts. Linjebus assesses that in the future, the traffic authorities will pay more attention to the working conditions of the bus operators' employees. Political attention is rising, and public transportation and the quality of public transportation are a much-discussed topic in Denmark. The traffic authorities are public institutions and Linjebus assumes that public institutions in the future will be forced to pay more attention to OSH when setting up the criteria for services; i.e. the traffic authorities have a direct impact on the bus drivers OSH when the traffic authority makes time schedules for the different bus lines.

Furthermore when Linjebus has won a contract, they include elements of the social accounts in the dialogue with the traffic authority. If, for example, improvement of time schedules are set up as a goal in the social accounts, dialogue with the traffic authorities about cooperation in projects improving the time schedules on specific bus lines would be opened.

Purchasers' experience

Major purchasers of Liniebus' service were asked if the social accounts have had any influence on the decision-making process selecting a bus operator.

The reply from the directors of three different traffic authorities shows that social accounts are given different market credit, from having no influence on the choice of bus operator to being a significant parameter.

One mentioned that due to political wishes, the final decision has so far been conditional on the lowest price, even though the tender material states 'Best value of price'. However, the director considers the social accounts as a very visionary and positive approach, which in the future might be weighted positively. Linjebus' concrete ways of specifying their goals are especially appreciated and both Linjebus' effort regarding OSH and ethnic minorities are praised. The director found the social accounts from Linjebus so remarkable that he forwarded the accounts to both the chairman and the deputy chairman of the board of the traffic authority.

Another mentioned that in their tender material, it is stressed that the OSH of the bus drivers is important, and documentation for how the bus operator ensured good OSH conditions should be presented when required. However, specific OSH requirements are not mentioned and a weighting system for which initiatives, OSH among others, are assessed as most important is not defined. The director thinks that social accounts are one way to illustrate that the bus operator takes OSH into consideration, and to indicate that the bus operator has a reliable attitude.

'The social accounts are public and the traffic authorities, who employ operators of public transportation, have an opportunity to give greater importance to the conditions for the employees in the contracted bus companies.'

Søren Clausen, Adm. Director for Linjebus. 19 April 1999

The third informed that they have defined a weighting system, which defines the credit given to bus operators documenting good performance regarding organisation and resources, and which also includes documentation of labour turnover and absence owing to sickness. As documentation of these issues the traffic authority evaluates the social accounts as a well structured and useful tool. The director mentioned that Linjebus' social accounts might have inspired the traffic authority to require that kind of documentation in the future.

Bus drivers' experience

A few bus drivers recently employed by Linjebus were asked if they knew about the social accounts and if they have had any influence on their decision being a Linjebus employee.

The answers showed that employees who were recently employed did not know about the social accounts, but were aware about specific OSH and social initiatives taken by Linjebus. One of the bus drivers mentioned that her perception of Linjebus was of a progressive bus operator with good communication between management and employees. She knew Linjebus as a bus operator who takes action when the bus drivers point out OSH problems. Also the personnel policy and the respect for each other were mentioned by another bus driver as the primary reason for choosing Linjebus as employer.

2.1.5. Impression of effectiveness and scale of application

In Denmark preparation of social accounts is a relatively new approach. The first social accounts were published in Denmark in 1999. It is the impression that social accounts are not yet a strong marketing tool. The customers are still not familiar with the social accounts and are seldom asking for them. However, the social accounts are foreseen to gain more attention in the future. Customers might to a greater extent become aware of the indirect influence of the working conditions on the quality of the product or service delivered and investors might to greater extent require information about a company's social behaviour. Social accounts and the process of establishing the accounts are seen as very useful in view of a company's internal social work, and if the social accounts are made, their use is an obvious marketing tool.

Using the social accounts, similar to those of Linjebus, as a marketing tool will probably be most efficient and applicable for service companies. When customers procure a service they (or their customers) get in direct contact with the one producing the service. Under these circumstances the importance of the working conditions for the one carrying out the service is most obviously of interest for the customer. Thus the Linjebus model of a social account is considered to be most useful for branches such as:

- transport operators;
- welfare work (i.e. care of elderly people);
- cleaning contractors;
- other branches carrying out services.

2.1.6. Further information

Further information regarding Linjebus' social accounts can be obtained from Project coordinator Jesper Lindeberg or Managing Director Søren Clausen, Linjebus A/S, Columbusvej 6, DK-2860 Søborg. Tel. (45) 43 42 07 00.

2.2 MARKETING OF ERGONOMIC HAND TOOLS — FISKARS

- Finland
- Product development tools
- Ergonomic qualities
- Product performance
- Documentation

2.2.1. Background

This case study describes some methods used for product development of ergonomic hand tools in relation to a project initiated by the Finnish company Fiskars. These methods have been used to document and motivate the marketing of non-powered hand tools as ergonomic in order to ensure the creditability of the company. Fiskars is generally known for quality, innovation and ergonomics represented by their products.

Non-powered hand tools constitute an important element of work and production systems. Hand tools are typically used in most jobs performed by the human operator. The demand for continuous improvement and increased knowledge in ergonomics creates the need for hand tools that are suitable for the required purpose. Occupational use of poorly designed hand tools has resulted in a great number of occupational disorders. These problems are every year the cause of great human suffering and economical losses all over Europe. Poorly designed hand tools cause an unnecessary workload and thereby decrease in productivity. There is a growing awareness in industry with respect to this correlation. Hand tools are also widely used during leisure time in activities such as gardening and construction. In North America and Scandinavia, ergonomics in tool design has become one of the major selling arguments. This implies growing dynamic markets for improved standard tools, and for new categories of specialised tools.

Fiskars manufactures a large number of garden tools. The garden tools are designed and developed with professional gardeners in mind. As an example tools are developed for winegrowers. In their job they carry out approximately one million cuts per season. However, tools are also developed for non-professional use, i.e. for being used by elderly people, who might have gnarled fingers and reduced muscular strength in their hands. In both situations it is very important that the ergonomics of the tool is optimised.

Fiskars has received several awards for products that are innovative, ergonomic, and feature the best industrial design, i.e. The American Rose Society (ARS) Endorsement and The Industry Forum Design Hannover (IFDH) Award. Fiskars uses these awards proactively in their marketing of the awarded products. Also other kinds of statements regarding the ergonomic properties of the products are used in Fiskars' marketing. When buying the pruners shown on the picture, a small pamphlet informs that the pruner is evaluated as the best in a survey of pruners carried out by the Tampere University of Technology. Additionally, the ergonomic properties are emphasised on Fiskars' home page with product presentations. The pruner is presented with the following text: 'And the rotating handle minimises strain and fatigue, especially during extended use'. Another pruner is presented with this text: ' PowerGear makes pruning much easier especially for gardeners with lower hand and arm strength'.

In order to support these statements, Fiskars needs proper documentation.

In the following, the methods to develop and document the ergonomic features of hand tools will be explained using the example of ergonomic gardening tools for winegrowers. The methods are developed or further developed in the EU-funded project titled 'Eurohandtool'.

One of the reasons for initiating the project was a 20–25 % absence due to sickness among pruners because of muscle disorders.

> The main objectives of the project were to:
> - improve the effectiveness, ergonomic quality and application areas of non-powered hand tools;
> - improve the productivity of work done by using them.

These objectives were reached by improving the hand tool mechanisms and design, developing better and faster evaluation methods for hand tool ergonomics, and developing better hand tool oriented work analysis methods.

In the 'Eurohandtool' project the main methods for task clarification have been a literature search, user questionnaires, theory of technical processes, the QFD method (quality function deployment) and a new method, the HTWAM method (hand-tool-oriented work-analysis method), developed by the German Darmstadt University of Technology. The Finnish Tampere University of Technology and Darmstadt University of Technology carried out the literature search. Tampere University of Technology produced user questionnaires.

These methods helped to carry through the project in a structured way in relation to the more unknown work processes performed by the winegrowers.

'Good products are always a compromise of a number of things, because everything has to be a compromise, but it is the best compromise in a way on the market, that's our goal.'

O. Lindén, Product Developer, Fiskars, Sweden

QFD is a planning tool which can be used to identify user requirements and transform the requirements to product attributes.

> *HTWAM is a general method used for total work analysis taking, e.g. working posture into consideration.*

The same set-up is not typically used in the daily development work at Fiskars. In general they find that the creative process should not be hampered by too many systems and they therefore look for more simple methods. Furthermore Fiskars base their development work on many years of experience, practical skills, intuition and less sophisticated modifications of the QDF method than used in the project.

2.2.2. Focus on occupational safety and health

The project focuses on ergonomics. Hand tools constitute an important element of work and production systems and the use of poorly designed hand tools in use has led to a serious increase of occupational disorders, such as Carpal Tunnel Syndrome and other cumulative trauma disorders.

For the whole development process of new products, design engineers need a thorough evaluation of tasks to be performed, working conditions and stress occurring in the specific workplace. This requires sound knowledge of ergonomics and of comparative job analysis data from different work tasks. This information can be used to identify workplace and product design priorities.

In the 'Eurohandtool' project data collection included the following steps.

<u>Literature search</u>

As the basic-level approach recommendations and limit values that already exist in the literature, standards and laws were used as a first way to evaluate the ergonomics of the hand tool. It is fast to perform and gives immediate feedback. However, this approach only gives answers for some characteristics concerning the mechanical and physical properties of a hand tool.

The design parameters are drawn from the above-mentioned data. Among other things, these data contains recommendations, limit values and background information about ergonomics related to specific parts of the hand tool.

Examples of design requirements:

<u>Interviews and questionnaires</u>

> *'The product concept always starts from the user demands. We have to be aware of the demands of the users, collect them and try to adapt to them as well as possible, keeping in mind that the price has to be reasonable and so on.'*
>
> O. Lindén, Product Developer, Fiskars, Sweden

The second step was to conduct interviews and send out questionnaires in order to have the users' opinions concerning tools, their preferred tool characteristics and their opinions. The interviews and the questionnaires were used to define user requirements. The respondents were asked about which factors were the most important for their selection of hand tools. The used questionnaire is available on the CD-ROM published as a part of the project.

Examples of user requirements:

User requirements	Explanation
Long-lasting and robust handles.	Handles do not bend, handles resist the abrasion of hands.
Surface of handles is comfortable, warm and does not abrade the hand or cause perspiration.	
Hand tool fits the hand. No part of it makes pressure on the hand.	
The grip span and the movements of the handles are suitable.	Track of the handles.
Opening of the blades is suitable.	Pruning shears are not suitable for branch thickness over 15–20 mm.
Hand tool is light to use.	Force transmission mechanism does not cause too much friction, the demand of force is small enough.
Locking mechanism is easy to use, reliable and can be operated by one hand.	
Blades are of good quality and retain their sharpness.	Blades do not crack, and must not be sharpened often.
Blades are not flexible sidewalks.	Branches and cuttings do not stay between the blades.

Quality function deployment

The QFD application was used to identify the areas where pruning shears, ergonomics could be developed. The main feature of the QFD is a correlation matrix model called the house of quality. With this model the user requirements are transformed into actions, by finding those design parameters having the greatest influence on the ergonomic quality of the hand tool.

The house of quality is the tool that allows user requirements to be compared with design parameters. The model gives information relating to how the available resources should be located to give the best response for users' needs. The product concept starts with collecting the user demands. These are adapted as well as possible, keeping in mind that the price has to be reasonable. The final product is always a compromise of a number of things, but the house of quality model is used to create the best compromise on the market. That is the goal. Each design parameter is given a target value. Technical difficulty and relative costs of design parameters have to be defined separately for each manufacturer. These factors are dependent on, for example, the manufacturers know-how and machinery and on the possible investments of a manufacturer, which must be made to attain certain improvements in products.

Example:

In the following example the correlation between user requirements and engineering variables are shown.

	Importance (score 1-10)	Engineering variables	Grip span	Grip span is optimal when force requirements is high	Length of handles	Grip force is tolerable	Friction between hand and handle	Heat transmission between hand and handle	No local pressure peaks	Blade sharpness	Friction between blade and branch	Blade opening	Good visibility to the cutting point	Color
Subjective user requirements														
Does not require high grip force				pos	pos	pos	pos				pos	pos		
Clean cut										pos				
Comfortable handle			pos		pos		pos	pos	pos					
Enduring									neg					
Good precision			pos		pos						pos	pos		
Possible to use gloves			pos	pos	pos									
Good looking			+		pos	pos			+			+	pos	pos
Technical difficulty														
Inputted importance (%)														
Estimated cost (%)														
Final targets														

The imputed importance of a design parameter was obtained by means of a sum product. The factors in this sum are the importance of a user requirement and the interaction correlation factor. The sums thus obtained are then added together for each design parameter.

Observations

In order to strengthen the QFD application the researchers observe the work done in an actual situation (field conditions) using a pre-selected analysis method. Based on reliable work analysing methods, a new method to analyse the work system with hand tools, the HTWAM, was developed during the 'Eurohandtool' project. Basically, the HTWAM method can be applied just using a paper checklist. For advanced evaluation of data input and the possibility to store the complete documentation of the analysed workplaces, the HTWAM checklist module has been computerised and is available on CD-ROM. The structure of the checklist and the focus items are shown in the following overview.

Structure	Items
1. Task	Duration/repetitiveness
2. Work objects	
Surface/size and weight	
3. Work equipment	
3.1. Kind of tool	Powered/non-powered kind of hand tool
3.2. Mechanical tool characteristics	Mechanical output/weight /centre of gravity/dimension
3.3. Grip characteristics	Span of grip/grip surface/workplace elements/working area
4. Work environment	
4.1. Physico-chemical environment	Lighting/climatic conditions/mechanical vibration/noise/sound/ hazardous substances
4.2. Accidents and health hazards	Health risks/body protection
4.3. Organisational environment	
4.3.1. Working hours and breaks	Working hours/breaks/interruptions
4.3.2. Remuneration / Work load	Basis of remuneration/work load/integration
5. Work demands	
5.1. Demands on the user	Body dimensions/training condition/hand size/hand strength/fine motor skills
5.2. Physiological factors	
5.2.1. Working posture	Back/arms/legs/head
5.2.2. Demands on precision	Fingers/hand-arm system
5.2.3. Static holding work	Finger-hand/hand-arm
5.2.4. Active light work	Arms and upper body muscles force/frequency Hand-arm system effort/frequency
5.2.5. Heavy dynamic work	Arms and upper body muscles force/frequency Legs and pelvic muscles force frequency
5.3. Psychomental factors	
5.3.1. Information reception	Perceptive accuracy/proprioreceptive information reception vigilance
5.3.2. Information processing	Professional experience
5.3.3. Information transmission	Working instructions/reactions/potential conflict situations

The items are pre-scaled in stress levels with a range from 0 to 5. A level of 0 represents very little stress, whereas level 5 means maximum stress for the user. The level as well as the time proportions of the stress is determined for each item. In the description of the HTWAM method each item has a brief description for all stress levels and common samples for accurate rating. There are various help functions to assist with data input. The analyst can retrieve data on standard examples, which help the analyst to make the correct HTWAM classification.

Additional information for complete documentation of the analysed workplaces can be input to visualise and facilitate the stress analysis like sketches or photographs of the workplace.

Besides the checklist, the HTWAM software consists of a number of additional modules facilitating the whole evaluation process, e.g. questionnaire report and 'job and stress profiles'.

Tests in field and laboratory testing

The 'Eurohandtool' project also used field and laboratory tests to evaluate specific elements of ergonomics. For example, in the case of pruning shears the tests were concentrated on force requirements, muscle load, blade configurations and handle friction.

Depending on the elements to be tested the testing methods varied from questionnaires to EMG for assessing muscle load and heart rate measurements.

A more sophisticated and comprehensive system was developed in the 'Eurohandtool' project. In the new system, EMG measurements as well as force and blade opening angle are included and can simultaneously be measured in order to obtain more complete information on the characteristics of the tool. By combining the results and by analysing the data using special computer software, this system gave insight into the forces and muscle activities required during different stages of cutting.

2.2.3. Current use of the scheme

Some of the methods used in the 'Eurohandtool' project are widely used. This regards interviews, questionnaires, the general laboratory tests, QFD and the house of quality model. However, combining the methods and supplementing them with a new observation analysis method, the HTWAM generates a new evaluation tool, which is still unique to the project. The HTWAM concentrated on using cutting hand tools in grape wine harvesting and tending grape wines, but the method has the potential to be easily adapted to all kinds of work which involves cutting or pruning hand tools, such as gardening, electrician and telephone linesman tools.

2.2.4. Experiences

The validation and reliability of the HTWAM method have been verified with existing analysing methods. The HTWAM method has been tested in field studies in different wine yards and has been modified and improved according to the test results. During this process, several items have been changed regarding definition and scaling of stress levels. In particular items for measuring ergonomic quality of the hand tool (e.g. grip characteristics) and heavy dynamic/static and active light work have been adjusted to the requirements of hand tools.

During 1997 and 1998 the HTWAM method has been verified to different analyses and workplaces. As a result, a standardised test method has been developed and applied. The data from several sessions with 5 to 6 test persons were processed in order to obtain advice relating to reliability. The test persons in the survey came from two different positions with respect to their experience in ergonomics and received an introduction in general aim/structure and application of the method. The analysis of workplaces with video sequences was done with workplaces/tasks, concerning tending grape wines. Also, different workplaces from wine growing, like a tiler workplace, have been analysed.

The persons who have developed the HTWAM method conclude that the application of the HTWAM method within the scope of the work system analysis is successful. The rating of visual impressions and the analysis of the work tasks carried out showed the essential stress factors. HTWAM makes it possible to identify weak points in a work system focusing on hand tools. HTWAM enables design engineers to prepare job stress and risk analyses which can be used to give advice on improved ergonomical design of hand tools to a company and to explain safety and health risk precautions to the users. Computerised stress registers will make it possible to give better services to companies developing hand tools in the future.

Supplier's experience

The hand tools developed for the winegrowers in accordance to the HTWAM are very promising, but Fiskars has not yet marketed the tools to the winegrowers. The weight of the developed hand tools, including the Fiskars Power Gear Pruner Pro, Fiskars Pull Saw, Fiskars Power Gear Lopper and a pouch to carry the tool, has been reduced to 0.890kg. from the conventional tool's 2.0 kg.

The use of the developed tool combination made the work faster with improved ergonomics as the total weight was reduced by 50 % from the previously used tool.

Regarding the new evaluation method, the fast way to analyse the ergonomic level of prototypes and a better way to get the feedback into design process has resulted in reduced time consumption and improved productivity.

Purchaser's experience

Since the new products have not been marketed yet, no responses from the specific target group are available. However, the prototype of Fiskars shears, developed within the project, was regarded as the best when compared with two commercial products in the subjective ratings given by the eight working people.

2.2.5. Impression of effectiveness and scale of application

The challenge facing the hand tool industry is quite big, but not insuperable. Although the problems are multifaceted no single system or solution exist. The industry is many times forced to rely on cumulated experience, knowledge of manufacturing processes and an innovative culture of the company in order to strive for continuous improvement in the design, production and marketing.

Regarding the use of the HTWAM method, Fiskars finds it very likely that this method can be applied in many areas where hand tools are used or even power-driven tools, e.g. agriculture, construction and assembling work.

The QFD method is especially applicable, because the engineer — the designer is often less familiar with the actual area and therefore needs a tool which quickly can point out the important criteria.

For many designers whose primary job is to develop quality products using experimental design and who are not necessarily interested in how the designs are constructed, Fiskars believe that the simple methods are the best approach.

2.2.6. Further information

More information about the 'Eurohandtool' project and the HTWAM is available at http://turva.me.tut.fi/euro/. The project is a BRITE_Euram project on Contract No BRPR-CT96-0350 entitled Eurohandtool/Project No BE96-3735.

The CD-ROM is available from Delta Industrie Informatic GmbH and via partner network (worldwide distribution channels: Malaysia, Netherlands, Spain, UK, US, etc.).

More information can also be obtained from Fiskars, FIN-10470 Fiskars. Tel. (358-19) 27 75 42; fax (358-19) 27 75 82. Contact person is Mr Torbjörn Lundmark

2.3 MARKETING OF OFFICE EQUIPMENT — KÖNIG + NEURATH

- Germany
- Integration of OSH in marketing
- OSH in product development
- Holistic view of OSH consultancy activities

2.3.1. Background

This case study describes the marketing strategy developed on the initiative of König + Neurath, a manufacturer of office furniture systems. A core objective of the marketing strategy is designing office workplaces to make them humane in the broad sense of the term. The company, which was founded in 1925, is today a worldwide operating manufacturer of office furniture with the highest turnover in Germany and one of the biggest manufacturers of office furniture in Europe. König + Neurath develops office furniture and room dividing systems and sells them through authorised specialist dealers. The specialist dealers are serviced by König + Neurath's distribution team.

König + Neurath applies the model of a holistic office concept developed from the optimum interplay of architecture, installation, ergonomics, function and design. The design principle of safety and health is intended to serve the adaptation of the working conditions to the individuals.

> König + Neurath's marketing states that:
> - its furniture is safe, harmless to health and a contribution to well-being at work on account of its consistent ergonomic and ecological requirements;
> - it offers individual, customised solutions for office workplace systems;
> - it is a one-stop provider of services and consultancy for the safe, humane and environmentally sound design of the office as a living space;
> - its furniture is adapted continuously to the changing requirements arising form the rapid change in forms of work.

2.3.2. Focus on occupational safety and health

König + Neurath has traditionally pursued a marketing strategy for their office furniture geared to safety and ergonomics. The company was, for example, in 1978 the first one to launch height-adjustable office desks onto the market. The safety and health oriented measures taken to implement the marketing strategy are product development, training and service.

Product development

In the development of product concepts, the aim is to take account of the most recent knowledge acquired in occupational medicine and the ergonomic requirements from the changing world of office work.

> Examples
> - Because of the considerable space required by 17-inch and even bigger monitors, there was a move away from standard sizes for working surfaces and new surface concepts were developed as shown in the picture.
> - For CAD [1] workplaces a desk with a tiltable screen section has been developed.
> - In order to avoid long-term sitting a desk has been developed which allows the dynamic change from sitting to standing by a 'lift-system'.
> - For the special requirements of call-centres special solutions are created.

Development of office furniture is conducted in multidisciplinary teams. These include for example physicians and ergonomists, occupational medical experts and engineers in ergonomics. User wishes are brought into the team through the distribution department and the specialist trade. Representatives of these

---
[1] CAD = computer aided design.

two groups meet in extra working sessions 2 or 3 times a year to exchange information.

Raw materials, as input to the office furniture, are purchased on the basis of a catalogue of criteria in accordance with the requirements of the eco-audit. The suppliers must confirm in writing compliance with the environmental requirements.

König + Neurath deals with customers' individual wishes, e.g. those arising from specific work sequences. For this purpose new solutions are developed in close cooperation with the responsible specialist dealer and the customer.

> Examples
> - A cupboard with a special baseboard was developed for a customer. This enabled him to move the cupboard when using a low-lift platform truck.
> - A specially designed small table was developed for a 'paperless office'.

Training

The members of the König + Neurath distribution team are trained as ergonomic consultants. This training is also offered to specialist dealers. In addition, König + Neurath offers its specialist dealers a training to qualify as 'workplace experts'. In this training many aspects of occupational safety and health at work are covered. König + Neurath subsidises participation in this external training by paying a substantial amount.

Via the Internet the trade, among other things, obtains supplementary information on ergonomics from König + Neurath.

Service

König + Neurath is working on the optimisation of CAD software, which automatically indicates critical issues in the planning process for example, the collision areas between the area of free movement and the functional area of furniture. The company offers specialist dealers seminars on the use of this CAD software.

König + Neurath gives support to entrepreneurs in achieving compliance with statutory requirements relating to the design of office workplaces, which are safe and harmless to health.

Through the specialist trade König + Neurath offers a comprehensive consultancy service on everything to do with offices, e.g. planning, facility management, and waste management.

> **Some examples**
> - Production and distribution of a manual with a compilation of and comments on laws, directives and standards with relevance to occupational safety and health at office workplaces.
> - Issue of practical guidelines ('Easy check') for assessing office workplaces with respect to the implementation of the requirements from the EU Framework Directive 89/391/EEC and the EU's VDU[2] Directive 90/270/EEC. The aim is to make complicated standard specifications easy to handle for non-specialists and to identify the actual need for consultancy.
> - Issue of a manual ('Office as living space') to help plan office workplaces. Aim: The planner is to see office workplaces as holistic work systems (including VDU work) and to observe all aspects of safety and health when planning office workplaces.

In collaboration with the specialist trade König + Neurath conducts training events in companies on demand, in order to explain to employees how to use the ergonomic benefits of the furniture.

2.3.3. Current use of application of the scheme

Observance of safety and health is binding specification of the company's management, but not one, which has been laid down in writing. Implementation is controlled in-house, by involving external experts, and partly through the eco-audit. The ergonomic quality of the sitting chairs is checked externally by an inspection institution and confirmed by a seal. About 350 specialist dealers are involved as multipliers. Approximately 35 000 copies of the manual for regulations and standards have been ordered, and approximately 170 000 of 'Easy check'.

2.3.4. Experience

No third party has evaluated the König + Neurath marketing strategy with respect to its basic health-oriented alignment and it's contribution to the market success.

Manufacturers' experience

The management of König + Neurath considers the consistent design of office furniture in accordance with safety and health protection as an essential prerequisite for market success. Moreover they are convinced that a comprehensive service range for the management of all aspects connected with the office is indispensable. In a rapidly changing world of office work and rising service wishes, a manufacturer of office systems must be able to react quickly and flexibly. He must have corresponding research and development capacities to produce appropriate furniture.

---

[2] VDU = visual display units.

The qualification of specialist dealers to perform competent consultancy work is in König + Neurath's experience a difficult task. König + Neurath adopts a top-down strategy and concentrates activities mainly on the key dealers. The purchase managers of large companies are often highly professional and set detailed ergonomic requirements. Dealers must be sufficiently qualified to approach this customer group. The training as ergonomic consultant, which König + Neurath offers to its dealers, is much in demand. It has therefore been necessary to subject to quotas.

Dealers' experience

One of the largest specialised dealers mentions, that he believes that the furniture from König + Neurath point the way forward in matters of safety and health.

It is the dealer's experience that customers rarely include ergonomic requirements when they ask for proposals. Furthermore the regulations often only contain minimum requirements, which do not take account of such ergonomically important aspects as the height adjustability of desks. This means that there is a major need for consultancy. For example to enable potential buyers to become convinced of this advantage and no longer base their choice on minimum requirements. The training given by König + Neurath to specialist dealer personnel to make them ergonomic consultants is a very helpful instrument from the dealer's point of view, and it has also proven valuable in motivating personnel.

Easy Check has prompted a great demand. Because of the dealer's own capacity bottlenecks, he has had to pass on consultancy enquiries to an external institute. The manual on regulations and standards has proven to be a sound work of reference for the dealer's interior architects.

The specialist dealer interviewed sees a weak point in the fact that customer companies are not willing enough to train their staff adequately in use of ergonomically sophisticated furniture. König + Neurath shares this view.

Experience of König + Neurath customers

A few customers of König + Neurath were questioned. An owner of a small company expressed great satisfaction with the furniture. It fulfilled his need for a large working surface in a small space as well as his wishes with regard to design, functionality, ergonomics, flexible use and durability. It was always possible to adapt the furniture to the different spatial conditions during the various moves of the company. The owner felt that he had received good advice from the specialist dealer. He was convinced that good workplace design, which creates a feeling of well-being, is generally a major motivating instrument for employees.

A purchasing manager from a large company with about 3 000 office workplaces reported that his company intended to redesign all office workplaces in accordance with the recent statutory requirements. An internal working group, which includes an occupational physician, had designed model workplaces for different working processes. Further tenders had been formulated with a detailed catalogue of requirements, also including aspects of safety, health and the environment. An order has been placed with König + Neurath and his specialist dealer. The purchasing manager stated that other

'We are continuously aiming to keep up to date by constant dialogue with work scientists, doctors and companies in the market and to react by adopting new approaches. That is one of our recipes for success.'

König + Neurath, interview

'König + Neurath has so far led the field in questions of ergonomics. For this reason and because König + Neurath is the market leader, we wanted to join the dealer network.'

Specialised dealer of
König + Neurath, interview

> 'König + Neurath offers very good advice and very good service. They look after the customer. They make every effort to comply with the special wishes of the customer.'
>
> Customer of König + Neurath

office furniture manufacturers make ergonomically good furniture. But König + Neurath differs from the competitors by the quality of its dealer network. Dealers' consultancy and service and accommodation to the wishes of customers with specifically customised developments are crucial.

The interviews with some users of König + Neurath desks revealed their satisfaction with the functionality, quality, appearance and ergonomic design of the furniture. The users assumed that attention was paid in their company to safety and health when selecting office equipment. Only one employee knew the brand name of her desk.

Some users reported that they had received adequate instruction in the use of the furniture. Others would have liked additional information. It seems that the height adjustment facility of a desk was not sufficiently exploited in the case of desk sharing.

2.3.5. Impression of effectiveness and scale of application

Safety and health in the design of office furniture has proven to be an essential prerequisite for market success. But this alone is not sufficient. The crucial factor is the incorporation of safety and health in a holistic approach to office work systems and a consequent holistic view of service. This means a consultancy-intensive strategy, whose consistent and broad-based implementation requires that a network of specialist dealers be set up, qualified and maintained. The approach thus adopted by König + Neurath seems to have contributed to the company's market success.

An adapted form of the König + Neurath strategy seems particularly suitable for companies whose products contribute to a healthy design of workplaces in various sectors. Companies who therefore also have to offer a humane, customised solution for the interface between the use of technical equipment and workplace furniture, for example:

- manufacturers of working tables in electrical engineering, precision mechanics, sewing companies or dental laboratories;
- manufacturers of cashpoint workplaces in supermarkets, dental laboratories.

Furthermore the König + Neurath strategy also seem applicable for manufacturers of working appliances which have to be designed with respect to safety and health, e.g. in the gardening domain. And for manufacturers of domestic furniture who wish to satisfy the growing demand for home office furniture.

2.3.6. Further information

Further information regarding the König + Neurath marketing strategy can be obtained from Marketing Communications Manager, Manfred Wuschanski, König + Neurath AG, Industriestraße 1, D-61184 Karben. Tel. (49-6039) 48 31 32; e-mail Manfred.Wuschanski@koenig-neurath.de

European Agency for Safety and Health at Work

2.4 MARKETING OF CAR CLEANING PRODUCTS — POLYTOP AUTOPFLEGE

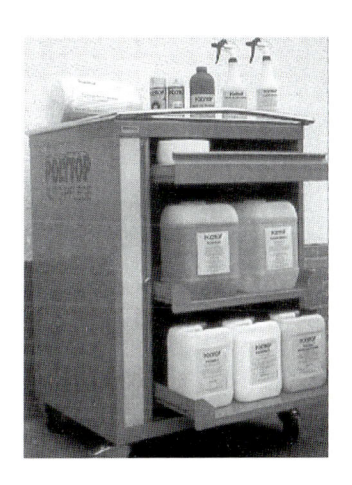

- Germany
- Integration of OSH into marketing
- Support for SMEs
- Product development
- Customer support

2.4.1. Background

This case study describes the support strategy the manufacturer Polytop Autopflege GmbH has developed for its customers, to protect them against health risks when handling chemical agents. Polytop is a small company which manufactures cleaning products and products to improve the appearance of used cars for the automotive sector and distributes them in Germany by its own sales force. Some of the products contain hazardous substances. The customers are so-called used car improvers, car sales companies and filling stations with car wash facilities. These are small companies. However there are also large car manufacturers among the buyers.

Polytop's management is in close contact with their customers. They therefore know that the customers – like most small companies – are hardly familiar with — and very often do not understand, the statutory requirements of the German Hazardous Substances Ordinance concerning protection against health hazards arising from dangerous agents. Customers frequently underestimate the health risks, which can emanate from hazardous substances and their unsafe use, and they hardly know anything about the health impact of hazardous substances on humans. Polytop has taken note of this and has integrated the safeguarding of customers' safety and health when handling chemical agents and environmental conservation in their marketing objectives and quality policy.

> Polytop marketing goals are:
> - to keep their competitive edge;
> - gain and retain the trust of customers by providing high, constant product quality, including as an elementary component compliance with health-related and ecological requirements; and by offering a comprehensive service in everything to do with car improvement. This service includes consultancy and support with respect to product application and procedures and the shaping of working conditions, also paying express regard to safety and health and support in the implementation of employer obligations in terms of occupational safety and health;
> - supply reliability;
> - an adequate pricing policy in relation to the range offered;
> - flexibility in adjusting the range to suit modern market needs, taking account as well of recent scientific knowledge on the environmental and health risk or compatibility of chemical substances.

2.4.2. Focus on occupational safety and health

Since 1996, Polytop has vigorously shaped a marketing programme with which safety and health-related information and services are integrated in all the suitable activities and channels of communication. Related principles have also been incorporated in its quality management in accordance with DIN EN ISO 90001. This marketing strategy encompasses the following fields.

Search of substitute substances: The aim of product development is the smallest possible health risk for users. This aim has also been integrated in the quality management. The products are therefore as far as possible manufactured on a water base. According to the company itself, Polytop is one of the few polish manufacturers who make no use whatsoever of aromatics. Solvents with low TLV (threshold limit value) are replaced as far as possible by alternatives with a higher TLV. Even if this necessarily means a higher market price in individual cases. In case of a conflict between achievable product performance and low health risk, one solution sometimes adopted is the inclusion of two product variants in the range: one with higher performance and greater health risk and one with lower performance and lower health risk potential. The company developed its own software for product development, in which warning features with regard to hazardous properties of chemical substances are incorporated and activated during the development processes in the case of risk.

Complete product package: Buyers of Polytop products have the guarantee that all products needed for the cleaning process meet environmental requirements. Full account is taken of the customer's desire for the minimum number of mutually adapted products in the improvement system. To supplement the basic demand for agents a skin protection range is offered as part of a skin protection plan.

Training of the sales force: New members of the sales force personnel undergo training where they are given, among other things, basic sales-relevant knowledge from the Hazardous Substances Ordinance and related legal fields.

Support for the entrepreneur to comply with legislation: Polytop informs the customers of their duties as employers with respect to drawing up operating instructions in their companies, and it supports customers by offering carefully formulated operating instructions for Polytop products. For the statutory labelling of small containers into which the Polytop products are poured from large containers in the buyer's facility, Polytop supplies appropriate labels showing the hazard symbols and labelling, the R and S phrases specified, safety instructions and water pollution classes. The carefully completed safety data sheets are passed on a disk as part of an information system, which contains among other things a list of all Polytop products with their exact identification. It therefore facilitates the statutory implementation of an index of hazardous substances.

Comprehensive service orientation: The service package includes consultancy and help on a wide range of topics and customer wishes. The support relates to linking the agents, the work equipment and the working environment. Work equipment is offered which helps in the use of the cleaning products. For this purpose a cooperation is established with other manufacturers, for example with a manufacturer of polishing machines, who has collaborated with Polytop to make a low-noise device, or with a complete supplier of protection equipment and fire safety appliances, or with a manufacturer who has developed especially light-intensive lamps for working in car interiors.

At Polytop strategies and appropriate activities are discussed and decided on against the background of the marketing objectives in a committee consisting of the managing director and those responsible for product development, production, process engineering and sales. The decisions are documented in written form.

2.4.3. Current use of application of the scheme

Polytop developed the approach described in the study on its own initiative, without the support of external institutions. With its specific form, this strategy is unique for such a small company. Due to the small size of Polytop and it's limited group of customers, the scope for action is restricted and the wider public is hardly aware of it. However, the basic principles and standards applied by Polytop are of general importance, and can therefore be transferred to other manufacturers of chemical products with the clientele of small enterprises.

2.4.4. Experience

No third party has evaluated the effect of the Polytop approach.

'We want to protect our customers as far as possible from the risk of injury through handling chemical agents by avoiding the use of hazardous substances in product development and providing assistance in product application. What is laid down in laws is not understood by medium-sized enterprises and cannot therefore be implemented. What is needed is a translator. We also see this as a gap in the market.'

Polytop, interview

Occupational safety and health in marketing and procurement

Manufacturers' experience

Polytop's management is convinced that the incorporation of safety and health in the marketing strategy and quality management contributes to long-term market success. This objective is supported by a sense of responsibility towards their customers. The company is aware that this strategy involves a greater effort in terms of development and that it takes up more time. In order to achieve a quick turnover, an aggressive pricing policy would be more effective. But management believes the approach adopted is forward-looking and creates enduring customer loyalty. Polytop people talk about positive reinforcing experiences.

Users of competitor products ask Polytop for help with problems concerning water pollution they encounter with the water authorities. As Polytop does not know the constituents of competitive products and the search for the substances that cause the effluent problems would cost a lot of analytical work, Polytop successfully offers its customers a guaranteed solution in the form of a complete switch to Polytop products.

Collaboration with some major car manufacturers is successful. Since these companies demand products which contain no hazardous substances or only a minimal amount and also the willingness to look for substitutes, Polytop has as a result of its product policy managed to be included in the list of some car manufacturers. Polytop is now even asked for as a problem-solver for these companies, the constant aim being a combination of a certain level of product performance and the principle of minimum health risks.

Recently the personnel in an automotive workshop belonging to an automobile company were so persuaded by a Polytop product that the head office decided to include the product in the automobile company's product range used worldwide.

According to the management personnel, the support activities Polytop offers its small customers to ensure that hazardous substances are handled without any health risk are also gratefully received and considered very helpful.

Experience of Polytop customers

'I have close ties with Polytop. All-round customer care is part and parcel of Polytop's service, e.g. relating to software for commercial matters and the treatment of water from the washing plant (Achtung: falls es sich hier um eine Autowaschanlage handeln sollte, bitte 'car wash' nehmen!!). That is very important for me.'

Customer, interview

Some Polytop customers were asked about their reasons for buying Polytop products and their attitude to the Polytop company. Results show that those questioned have a close relationship with Polytop and its products. This is based on the confidence they feel towards the reliable product quality and on the comprehensive advice and support they get for varied car improvement problems. They think this puts Polytop in a class of its own. By product quality, the customers mean a constant, high product performance. Health aspects play a secondary role for them when they select a product. But these customers are convinced that Polytop use as few hazardous substances as possible. This is also backed up by the fact that the products are on the lists of the car manufacturers with their rigorous safety, health and environmental standards, manufacturers for whose franchise workshops the customers questioned work. Customers believe that Polytop is comparable in this respect with other good manufacturers.

The support facilities in the area of hazardous substances, such as operating instructions, labelling, the information system is familiar. Not all the customers questioned make use of these aids. Their behaviour in this respect depends on the basic attitude of the company owner towards occupational safety and health. One informant referred to his boss's tendency to reject anything to do with occupational safety and health. In contrast, another entrepreneur reported that a Polytop salesman had even conducted an occupational safety and health course in his company. Since then the company itself has conducted the statutory courses.

'If you have problems with a product, e.g. if the polish does not work properly, the Polytop people react immediately. You even have a direct line to the product developer.'

Customer, interview

2.4.5. Impression of effectiveness and scale of application

Many studies have demonstrated that small entrepreneurs need help in order to handle hazardous substances without causing health risks. Manufacturers and dealers are the most important reference points and sources of information for small companies with regard to the chemical products used. They thus play a key role in consultancy, but without always fulfilling their responsibility. Polytop's strategy therefore meets an objective need. The broad approach adopted by Polytop, ranging from product development, through information and support in application to the equipment, meets this need within the possibilities a small manufacturer has for exerting an influence on his customers. Small entrepreneurs are confronted in day-to-day practice with a wealth of tasks and problems with tight human and financial resources. Questions of occupational safety and health therefore play a relatively secondary role in everyday operations.

Adaptation of the strategy adopted by Polytop for helping customers when handling hazardous substances seems particularly appropriate for producers of chemical products, whose main customers are small-sized companies and who feel responsible for protecting their customers' health. Thus the Polytop approach is evaluated as being most suitable for manufacturers of:

- agents used for cleaning buildings;
- paints and lacquers;
- products for the hairdressing trade;
- agents for various construction trades, such as roofers, heating, sanitation and air-conditioning engineers, etc.

2.4.6. Further information

Further information regarding the Polytop approach can be obtained from the Managing Director, Markus Obermeyer or from the Product Developer, Theo Lorenz, Polytop Autopflege GmbH, Vor der Pforte 17, D-63303 Dreieich. Tel. (49-6103) 840 11; e-mail info@polytop.de

2.5 MARKETING IN EMPLOYMENT SERVICE SECTOR — VEDIOR BIS

- France
- Protection of temporary workers
- Prevention
- Communication and marketing policy
- Safety used as a commercial strength

2.5.1. Background

The issue: The growth of temporary work (470 000 full-time job equivalents in 1999 in France) is continuous. This leads to negative effects on occupational safety and health, since temporary employees are less integrated into the user firm than permanent employees. Temporary workers have higher than average accident rates. BIS company is one of the first large firms to have reacted to this development. The alert was given in 1994 when large chemicals groups decided to no longer make use of temporary workers given the risks specific to their industry. BIS had to face this challenge and develop an appropriate response to the problem of occupational safety, fitting in with a sales approach. BIS became the safety partner of its customers by training its temporary workers in safety, giving them a specific safety culture so that they can remain safe even when they change firm. This method, adapted to the use of temporary workers was being rewarded in 1996 by an AISS prize. In September 1997, BIS joined the Vedior BIS group. This policy of occupational safety was then not only maintained but even reinforced.

Key points:
- establish a permanent concern for safety among temporary personnel, by developing a specific occupational safety culture;
- have this safety culture shared by the customers through continuous, precise analysis of workstations, taking into account safety and health criteria;
- create tools for the agencies, which integrate safety into a sales approach designed to promote awareness of this subject by both the temporary worker and the user firm.

Objective: Eliminate fatal occupational injuries, reduce the rates of accident frequency and severity and make the concern for ensuring the safety of temporary workers in the user firm an essential aspect. This approach is based on participation, calling on the sense of responsibility of all the players in the work assignment process.

Means: A strategy, which makes safety a marketing instrument. The financial aspect is not overlooked. The cost of occupational injury contributions is high, and a reduction in this cost would have an impact on overall group profits. This strategy is also based on the attention from the agency personnel for their temporary workers. A department in Lyons is responsible on the national level for preparation and management of the tools made available to the local agencies. These tools include a manual of work assignment procedures and instruction materials.

> 'Within Vedior BIS there is a willingness to have no fatal accidents.'
>
> Mr J. Messina — Head of Safety Department

2.5.2. Focus on occupational safety and health

Criteria: Vedior BIS has 650 agencies and 3 000 permanent employees. Between 400 000 and 600 000 temporary work assignments are performed annually, representing the equivalent of 90 000 full-time employees. In 1994 28 000 accidents with job stoppage including 24 fatal accidents, were counted in France for all temporary work assignments.

Parameters: The elimination of fatal job injuries is the ultimate objective. This is an important aspect of the corporate culture. A constant decline in the rate of accident frequency and severity is also sought. Each agency knows its results and the cost represented by its accidents. These rates are management instruments because the temporary work firm is the employer of the temporary employee.

> 'Some agency managers resigned after having experienced a fatal accident within their temporary work force.'
>
> Mr J. Messina — Head of Safety Department

2.5.3 Current use of the scheme

Scope: The scope is to manage the integration of temporary workers into the user enterprise in a safe manner. The approach is to create a safety culture, make it operative and ensure that it persists for both customers and temporary workers. A specific department, based in Lyons and reporting directly to senior management, is in charge of this. It comprises two entities, one administrative and the other in charge of prevention and occupational risks. The main role of the administrative unit is to establish a statistical database from occupational injury reports. This base, being built since 1996, traces the history of accidents. This data is used by the other unit, whose role is to develop the tools made available to the agencies, to check the correct use of these tools and to develop the system. The group's strategy is implemented on the local level by 35 regional coordinators.

Operation: This policy has a cost, which is considered as a marketing investment offset by the savings made on contributions. Given the large payroll managed by the firm, the amount of this reduction in contributions is significant.

This strict work assignment procedure comprises several aspects.

For some jobs such as those of construction machinery operators, Vedior BIS goes further than the legislation requires and demands a minimum of experience in a company.

<ins>Know the temporary workers:</ins> The job interview is carried out using a guide which includes a questionnaire concerning, among other things, the elementary safety principles that the candidate must know depending on the job he claims to know. If the candidate does not have this basic knowledge, he will not be assigned but advised to take a training course.

A personal document is handed to each temporary worker assigned. There are two types of booklets. The 'safety passport' in which the basic safety principles are recalled, for assignments to customers in jobs in which there is no particular risk, such as secretarial tasks. If there is greater risk, a 'welcome booklet' will be supplied. The handing over of this booklet is formalised by a signature from the temporary worker, emphasising the importance of the information contained in the booklet.

<ins>Know the customer:</ins> An analysis of the risks present at the workplace is performed by Vedior BIS before any job assignment in cooperation with the user firm. It is of fundamental importance to know and visualise the workplace to be able to inform temporary workers of the conditions in which they will perform their work. In this workplace study, a precise definition is given of the work to be performed. Possible malfunctions are listed there, with their consequences and especially with the actions to be taken to remedy them. The physical environment and the work environment are also described. The user firm commits itself to this document by signing it.

This field work enables Vedior BIS to write the customer a 'welcome booklet', already mentioned, which is handed to the temporary workers. Vedior BIS produces this booklet in cooperation with the customer and all the risks are analysed in it. This booklet can be specific to the customer in the case of a large account or correspond to a specific industry in the case of a specific activity for an occasional customer. Also Vedior BIS's permanent personnel receives in-depth training, being taught to recognise and measure risks, which makes the analyses of work stations pragmatic and efficient. These analyses form an integral part of sales prospects. Vedior BIS extends its activities to the role of consulting without this involving the assignment of personnel.

The determination not to assign staff without a precise knowledge of the workplace is interpreted as a sign of dependability by customers. Vedior BIS also wants to know whether a customer is not looking to transfer a risk to it. Customers not respecting the regulations or refusing to adapt to them are ruled out. When an accident occurs, a joint analysis is carried out to draw all possible lessons from it and define safety improvements to be made in this customer's enterprise. This facet of Vedior BIS's action will soon be reinforced to increase its effectiveness.

<ins>The station entry sheet:</ins> Each job assignment is followed up, and the actual conditions of the assignment are analysed and recorded. For regular customers these documents are condensed in a summary handed to the user firm, thus giving it feedback on its image.

<ins>Communication instruments ensuring the sustainability of this action:</ins> The messages are adapted to the target group, as for example the 'safety booklet'

associated with a 'safety game' designed for students doing temporary work during the summer and for whom this is often their first contact with the work environment. Safety training is provided for temporary workers at the agency level by its permanent staff with appropriate instruction materials. Whenever a particular or new risk is encountered, for instance by a new customer, a specific training package is developed.

To ensure the sustainability of the promotion of safety awareness, Vedior BIS has recently organised events on the theme 'Let's play safe'. This involves bringing together temporary workers and current or future customers for a day to outline and discuss safety. All those players having a message to put across are involved in these events. Attention is paid to the speakers and the demonstrations during the day end with a competition and prize-giving ceremony.

Control: This system functions with strict procedures. All the agencies are audited twice a year to check their good implementation of the procedures explained in this report. The safety test to be passed by temporary workers and the workplace study in the customer's enterprise are two compulsory stages in the assignment procedure. Any failing is punished severely. As legal employer, the agency manager is responsible in the event of an accident. Compliance with the Vedior BIS internal procedure ensures him of the legal support of his senior management in the event of legal action.

2.5.4. Experiences

Originality: This proactive policy helps keep control over work assignments. It combines light and serious aspects and imposes constraints going further than required by the rules, such as the refusal to assign workers when the appropriate conditions are not met.

The enterprise uses the theme of safety integral to the personnel assignment service in its marketing action. A 'safety' sales representative maintains a prevention dialogue with the large accounts.

Experience of buyers: For a large firm the use of temporary staff is often a necessity. The reliability of the temporary work firm is an assurance of a quality service. Vedior BIS provides this service through its knowledge of the jobs for which it assigns staff, the workplace, its temporary workers and its customers. More specifically this firm's network includes agencies specialised in construction and public works managed by former workers in the sector. The cost of this service is not really higher than elsewhere, and it enables the user firm to supply its own customers within the deadlines, complying with the required quality criteria. The Vedior BIS temporary workers know their job and the procedures of the user firm. In its business, Vedior BIS is a precursor in safety which is able to stay ahead because its method works. It is therefore imitated by its competitors. This is the analysis made by Bouygues, one of the European construction majors. Bouygues attaches great importance to the safety of its personnel, and its results are among the best in the industry. It is the Vedior BIS policy which attracted the attention of Bouygues. Sales relations take the form of a framework contract at the national level and at the regional level. This contract governs sales relations and provides for follow-up including a major section on safety, such as, for example, accident analysis and the taking of corrective measures.

Bouygues is well aware that the cost of non-safety in its temporary workers' supplier will be invoiced to it. This is why it works in partnership with Vedior BIS to improve the training modules for temporary workers and agency managers and adapt them to the new Bouygues's working procedures. In exchange, the temporary workers will be received with closer attention at Bouygues. It is also considered that the assignment of under-qualified personnel in the construction industry will soon be no longer possible given the increasing complexity of this industry.

2.5.5. Comments on the effectiveness of the system

This resolute prevention action lowered the rate of accident frequency by 40 % and the rate of severity by 35 %. This decline has been continuous for about three years in most agencies. The accident rate for temporary workers at Vedior BIS is thus 35 % lower than the industry average. As already mentioned, the investment cost is largely offset by lower rates of contribution.

The accident frequency and severity rates are available to any temp companies so they can evaluate their performance by using these rates. The basic principles of this scheme, such as the knowledge of the customer and of the worker, are also transferable to other temp companies. If the large companies will be able to have a global safety policy the small ones specialised on a very specific branch of industry will have to focus their action on the specificities of their clients.

Work place studies and knowledge of everything relating to occupational safety and health, places Vedior BIS among the experts capable of helping the firm make work safer. Vedior BIS has already carried out corporate safety audits, until now on a one-off basis. This real, tangible experience will soon be placed at the disposal of enterprises, as Vedior BIS is creating a division dedicated entirely to consulting and occupational safety audits.

2.5.6. Further information

Mr Joseph Messina Vedior BIS, Head of the Safety Department, 120 Rue Masséna F-69006 Lyons. Tel. (33) 472 83 26 42; fax (33) 472 83 26 29; e-mail: joseph.messina@vediorbis.com

3.

OSH IN GENERIC MARKETING SYSTEMS

3.1 MARKETING OF BUILDING PRODUCTS — INDOOR CLIMATE LABELLING SCHEME

- Denmark
- Label
- Building product quality
- Marketing tool
- Purchasing tool

3.1.1. Background

This case study describes a voluntary indoor climate labelling scheme. The scheme was developed by The Danish Society of Indoor Climate in 1995 on the initiative of The Danish Ministry of Housing. To issue and supervise the label certificate an association called The Danish Indoor Climate Labelling was established in order to have a normative and an issuing part. The labelling scheme is intended for building products and other products influencing the indoor air climate.

> The purpose of the indoor climate labelling scheme is to improve the indoor air climate in buildings by:
> - providing users with a tool for the selection of more indoor friendly building products;
> - providing a tool for better understanding of the impact of building products on indoor air;
> - providing manufacturers with a tool to develop more indoor friendly building products.

Since 1995 requirements and test standards have been developed for the following product groups:

- ceiling and wall systems;
- textile flooring;
- interior doors and folding partitions;

- resilient floorings, laminated floors and wood-based floors;
- oils for wooden floors;
- windows and exterior doors;
- kitchen, bath and wardrobe cabinets.

Still more product groups will be included in the future, i.e. interior building paints, cleaning agents and furniture.

Working groups, appointed by The Danish Society of Indoor Climate, develop the requirements and the test standards. Each working group has approximately 15 members representing the manufactures, suppliers, trade organisations, R & D institutions and The Danish Indoor Climate Labelling. A hearing is organised before the final approval the draft product standard group. This hearing involves relevant suppliers, which are not directly involved in the product standard work, such as: trade organisations and other interested parties, as authorities, testing laboratories, indoor air scientists, product specialists and professional users according to procedures used in other international standardisation.

The test and labelling criteria of the Danish Society of Indoor Climate are described in two kinds of standards: standard test methods and product standards. the basic frame of the testing and labelling criteria is given in the general 'standard test methods' and the product specific criteria are given in the 'product standards'.

In the latest Danish building code (1995), the indoor climate labelling scheme is recommended to be used (Danish building code, Ministry of Housing and Building in Denmark; Copenhagen 1995).

The aim of the indoor climate labelling scheme is to ensure healthy buildings without allergens.

3.1.2. Focus on occupational safety and health

The indoor climate label focuses on the following relevant indoor climate issues:

- de-gassing of chemicals;
- particle emission (only required for ceiling systems);
- guidelines for projecting, storage, transportation, installation, use, cleaning, maintenance, etc.

Regarding de-gassing, the specific indoor-related time-value is determined on basis of measurements of the chemical emission of single volatile organic substances combined with sensory evaluation of odour from a newly manufactured product. The indoor-related time-value, describes how long a product will emit compounds that may cause odour and mucous membrane irritation. To phrase it popularly, the indoor-relevant time-value is the time it takes from a product being installed to a point when the emissions of all single substances have reached an acceptable concentration in the indoor air. A declared time-value of, for example, 10 days means that the probability of the product to cause odour or to cause irritation in eyes, nose and upper respiratory passage is insignificant later than 10 days after installation of the product.

For ceiling systems an examination of the particle emission is carried out in excess of emission testing (indoor-relevant time-value). Emission of particles from ceiling systems are determined by sedimentary dust consisting of particles including fibres, which could cause irritation on skin or in eyes, nose or upper respiratory passage in the first period after installation. Emission of particles including fibres is divided into three classes:

- low emission of particles less than or equal to 0.75 mg/m^2;
- medium emission of particles larger than 0.75 mg/m^2 and less than or equal to 2 mg/m^2;
- high emission of particles larger than 2 mg/m^2.

For ceiling systems an emission of particles corresponding to low or medium gives the right to label according to the indoor climate labelling.

The suppliers holding the indoor climate label are obliged to prepare indoor-related guidelines for transport, storage, installation, cleaning and maintenance in order not to decrease the indoor air properties during the total time of use of a product, when used as intended.

The indoor climate labelling has a defined scope to expand to cover other indoor-related properties than chemical and sensory emission, particle emission, and guidelines. R & D projects provide continuous improvement and developments of the indoor climate labelling. When generally accepted indoor air threshold values concerning carcinogenic and allergenic effects are defined, these health effects are expected to be included. Additionally, it can be decided to include other indoor-related properties in specific product areas, if properties and test methods are well defined.

3.1.3. Current use of application of the scheme

The indoor climate label is today available in Denmark and Norway. Sister organisations to the Danish Society of Indoor Climate and The Danish Indoor Climate Labelling have operated in Norway since 1998. An international committee, with Danish and Norwegian participation, takes care of the international coordination with regard to common technical standards and labelling conditions. The international organisation is prepared for further international extension. At the moment negotiations are ongoing with a number of countries.

Each certificate covers a specific product group manufactured or imported by the company and each product group includes products with an identical indoor climate performance. At present 34 product groups with more than 300 products are marketed with the indoor climate label in Denmark and Norway.

Approximately 100 manufacturers have a certificate allowing them to use the indoor climate label.

3.1.4. Experiences

No third parties have evaluated the scheme.

In 1999 the Danish Society of Indoor Climate evaluated the scheme in order to give a status and transfer knowledge to the on-going work within the society.

According to this society, trade organisations and individual companies often mention that the close collaboration between manufacturers, distributors, trade organisations and the indoor climate labelling organisations as well as the labelling criteria balancing the indoor air properties and the technical performance of the products, are crucial for the industrial commitment.

According to the Danish Society of Indoor Climate, professional users in Denmark and Norway have emphasised the importance of the fact that the indoor climate label is scientifically based and that the result can be given as one single indoor-relevant time-value. Provided that proper information is available, this time-value is easily understood and can easily be used for comparison between products within the same category of use. Manufacturers who have used the indoor climate label scheme mention that the concept — and specifically the chemical emission with analyses of all important single volatile organic compounds in the emission — is an operational tool that enables manufacturers to include indoor air properties in their product development. Also the dynamic aspect of the indoor climate label that product improvements are immediately shown in the indoor-relevant time-value is important for both manufacturers and users.

Although there still is a small number of labelled products, the society assesses that the indoor climate labelling work influences the manufacturers' product development and users' product selection specifications towards the goal of improving the indoor air quality in buildings. Even manufacturers — who have decided that the time is still not ready for labelling or declaration of indoor air properties of their products — have in several cases used their knowledge from e.g. the indoor climate label product standard work to improve their products considerably with regard to indoor air.

Suppliers' experience

The technical manager at a Danish company — Rockfon A/S, which uses the indoor climate label proactively in their marketing, was interviewed. The Technical Manager is head of the product development and is organisationally placed in the Marketing Division. Rockfon A/S is part of the Rockwool International Group and is one of the largest manufactures of ceiling systems presented on most European markets.

Rockfon A/S has from the very beginning participated in the working group developing the requirements and the test standards for ceiling systems. According to the Technical Manager, Rockfon A/S expected that their competitors would apply for the indoor climate label and in order to secure the company's Danish markets shares Rockfon A/S decided to participate in the working group. Rockfon A/S also found it crucial to participate in order to become aware of potential initiatives as early as possible, and to influence the results.

At present Rockfon A/S has obtained the indoor climate label for all their product lines manufacturing ceiling systems. The ceiling systems could without any specific product development fulfil the indoor climate label criteria. When new products are developed, the indoor climate label criteria are used to guide the product development. In-house laboratory tests are carried out during the development process in order to control that the final product can pass those third party laboratory tests required for obtaining the indoor climate label. Rockfon A/S also uses the indoor climate criteria to set up requirements to their suppliers. Supply control is carried out within an existing system for controlling intermediate products. The technical manager assesses the scheme as non-bureaucratic and he stated that small companies as well as large would find it useful to introduce the indoor climate label and to join a society like the Danish Society of Indoor Climate.

The indoor climate label provides more specific information than a simplified label, as the specific indoor-relevant time-value is declared.

Rockfon A/S assesses the indoor climate labelling scheme as an appropriate marketing tool. Especially the company is pleased that a uniform standard of comparison between different products was introduced by establishing the indoor climate labelling standard test methods. Furthermore, the indoor climate label provides more specific information than a simplified label, as the specific indoor-relevant time-value is declared. Thus, the users are informed not only about whether a product has obtained the indoor climate label or not, but also if the product has a performance classified among the best, the middle or the poorest of these products fulfilling the indoor climate criteria.

Rockfon A/S would like the indoor climate labelling scheme to become more widespread. If the scheme was established in more countries, the competition on these markets would also include the product's indoor climate performance resulting in an improved level of the indoor climate. With the scheme established only in Denmark and Norway, the technical manager thinks that the scheme primarily serves to prevent dumping the level in these countries. All Danish manufactures offer ceiling systems that are indoor climate labelled in the best class and the customers demand these labelled products. Within other product groups, as for examples textile flooring, the technical manager believes that non-labelled products or products not classified in the best class might still be on the Danish market. Within these product groups there is still room for obtaining credit for better product developing.

Purchasers' experience

The professional purchasers have been asked whether they require that the contractor use building products, which are indoor climate labelled. The professional purchasers are in this context understood as the one projecting the buildings for the building owners.

The users are informed if the product has a performance classified among the best, the middle or the poorest of these products fulfilling the indoor climate criteria.

The responses indicate that it is not a widespread practise to set up requirements regarding the indoor climate label. However, the most proactive architects and planners do require indoor climate labelled products. Indoor climate labelled products are especially requested when building schools and other public institutions. For instance the Danish Ministry of Research requires indoor climate labelled products or products fulfilling the conditions given by the indoor climate label when they are the building owner. The architects and planners believe that the indoor climate label will become more in demand in the future. The architects and planners perceive a growing interest in health and environmental issues from the Danish public building owners and housing associations.

When asking if the indoor climate products are more expensive than similar not labelled products the responses differ. One respondent believes that the prices are the same whether the product is labelled or not. Another respondent stated that contractors have a tendency to let every requirement follow by an increase in price. However, he was not certain that the price increase was due to higher prices on the indoor climate labelled products, it might as well be a psychological reaction.

3.1.5. Impression of effectiveness and scale of application

It is the impression that the indoor climate labelling scheme has an impact on the development of more indoor climate friendly building products. The influence of the label would probably be more significant if new product groups should be included. The non-bureaucratic cooperation between manufacturers and scientists and others when establishing the requirements and the test standards ensure well-balanced criteria. However, the manufactures might influence the criteria so that they are not too difficult to fulfil. Thereby the indoor climate labelling scheme could be a driving force for product development primarily when new product groups are included by the labelling scheme and when the criteria are revised. If the labelling scheme is introduced in countries, where manufactures have difficulties fulfilling proposed criteria, there is a risk, that these manufactures will influence the criteria settings and promote less ambitious criteria and hereby reduce the positive effect of the indoor climate label.

The list of certified Danish manufacturers and importers has been analysed. The list includes primarily medium sized companies. The distribution is:

- 1 % with 1–10 employees;
- 7 % with 11–20 employees;
- 16 % with 21–50 employees;
- 25 % with 51–200 employees;
- 5 % with 200–1 000 employees;
- 1 % with more than 1 000 employees;
- 44 % without any information about the number of employees.

An initiative similar to the Indoor Climate Label might be applicable as a motivating force for development of more indoor climate friendly products if:

- manufacturers believe that fulfilling the requirements result in enlarged market shares;
- the users are concerned about the existing products influence on the indoor climate;
- the users' concerns can be communicated in common demands, i.e. through key persons as architects and consulting engineers setting standard requirements for building products i.e. in tender materials.

3.1.6. Further information

Further information regarding the scheme, membership, initiation of new products, standard groups, status of the standardisation work and new literature can be obtained from: The Danish Society of Indoor Climate, Ms Anne-Lise Larsen, Danish Technological

Institute, Postbox 141, DK-2630 Taastrup. Tel. (45) 43 50 42 38; fax: (45) 43 50 40 24; e-mail: annelise.larsen@teknologisk.dk. More information about the scheme might also be found at the following home page: http//www.dsic.org/dsic.htm.

More information about Rockfon's experiences using the indoor climate labelling scheme in their marketing, can be obtained from Technical Manager Vagn Boe Hansen, Rockfon A/S, Hovedgaden 501, DK-2640 Hedehusene. Tel. (45) 46 56 21 22

3.2 MARKETING OFFICE EQUIPMENT — THE TCO LABELLING SCHEME

- Sweden
- Proactive trade union initiative
- Marketing on basis of well-documented OSH performance
- Label — an easy aid to purchasers
- Increased market shares for companies fulfilling the requirements

3.2.1. Background

This case describes the voluntary TCO labelling scheme. The scheme is introduced by the trade union TCO (The Swedish Confederation of Professional Employees).

> The purpose of the TCO label is to:
> - stimulate the manufactures to develop more occupational and environmental safe office equipment.
> - assist purchasers to choose office equipment less problematic for the users and the external environment.
> - provide the purchaser as well as the vendor with a clearly defined label, and hereby saving time, work and cost in the purchasing process.

In the beginning of the 1980s, TCO realised that personal computers were going to be the primary tool for the 1.3 million members in the TCO association. At the same time, the first concerns began concerning a possible connection between magnetic fields, foetal damage and pregnancy problems. Shortly after, other terms such as electromagnetic hypersensitivity during work with computers, computer stress and physical strain injuries became common.

On this background, TCO decided to draw up and set requirements together with user representatives and technical experts – and to address the requirements directly to the market. This brought about a completely new form of trade union influence. As TCO puts it, this new trade union initiative speeded up a previously slow and cumbersome method where it took years for the authorities to issue regulations to prevent health-endangering work. With the TCO initiative, close cooperation with ambitious manufacturers laid foundation for rapid and efficient product development.

The first TCO label was introduced in 1992 (TCO'92). Two more labels have been introduced in 1995 and in 1998 with still more intensified requirements and including still more product groups.

TCO'92 introduced requirements for reduced electric and magnetic fields, energy efficiency and improved electrical safety. The label guaranteed compliance with the requirements. Manufacturers had a vested interest in showing that their products met the requirements of TCO'92, and TCO's members wanted their purchasing to be simplified.

Three years later TCO'95 permitted complete computer equipment to be labelled with quality and environment guarantees; not just the display, but also keyboards, system units, flat screens and portable computers became subject to the requirements. Over and above the TCO'92 demands, ecological and ergonomic/functional requirements were added.

In October 1998, TCO'99 was introduced to the market, being a revised version of TCO'95 to the extent that the requirements cover the same range of products plus alternatively designed ergonomic keyboards. The requirement areas are the same but with TCO'99 the requirements have been further tightened and a number of new ones added. Additionally, the TCO'99 includes more products — printers, faxes, copiers. Many of the requirement areas and criteria are identical, but other parts are new for these product groups, i.e. requirements for the equipment to be better adapted for use by the 20 % of the work force who have some kind of physical disability.

For each product group a report exists informing about the requirements and their associated test methods for certification in accordance with the label. Third party verification by accredited laboratories is required for the majority of demands.

3.2.2. Focus on occupational safety and health

Among the requirements relevant to the safety and health of the employees, the TCO'99 include requirements regarding:

- Image refresh rate (avoiding display flicker);
- visual ergonomics;
- magnetic and electric fields;
- display image stability;
- rapid restart after power down;
- heat emission;
- noise level;
- chemical emissions;
- keyboard design.

The TCO labelling scheme has become a major factor in the technological development of display units.

Additional requirements for printers, faxes and copiers include placing and identification of control buttons, alternative versions of control functions, easy access, i.e. if paper jams occur, and requirements of user manuals to be in the local language.

The requirement specifications have been drawn up by TCO in cooperation with the Swedish Society for Nature Conservation, The Swedish National Energy Administration and SEMCO AB and in direct dialogue with OSH and environmental experts, users, manufacturers and trade experts.

3.2.3. Current use of the scheme

The TCO quality and environmental labelling schemes are today global standards. The reports informing about the requirements and the associated test methods are available in both Swedish and English. TCO has agreements with 100 manufacturers worldwide and more than 900 display models have been certified to TCO'92, whereas over 1 000 have the TCO'95 approval. Also a large number of displays, a limited number of system units and one single keyboard have already achieved the TCO'99 label.

3.2.4. Experiences

The TCO labelling scheme has been evaluated in 1998 in an EU's DG XIII financed Sphere+ project [3]. The author states that he feels rather confident that the TCO labels have been a big success. During 1998 some 90 million display units were sold worldwide. One third of those were TCO labelled. As a consequence of this dominating position plus the tough and rising demands, the TCO labelling scheme has become a major factor in the technological development in this area. According to the author, electromagnetic fields have been reduced by more than a factor 10, flicker and energy use have been sharply reduced and TCO's work in setting standards for the visual ergonomics has opened up for increased endeavours in the field of organisational redesign for the work environment. The author highlights, as a specific conclusion, that turning unions from reactivity to pro-activity, and threatened members from victims to active forces of change, contains the most important lesson to draw from the TCO labelling scheme.

TCO development assesses that the scheme has contributed to a more concentrated focus on technical development of user requirements, a better working environment and concurrently reduced load on the external environment. Furthermore, the companies and organisations are regarded as winners because they have an increased awareness of what good equipment means in terms of increased productivity and lower costs. Other beneficiaries are producers and manufacturers of the equipment, who project themselves in front in technical development and thereby improve their competitiveness.

'There are more winners. Companies and organisations now have a heightened awareness of what good equipment means in terms of increased productivity and lower costs. Other beneficiaries are also the producers and manufacturers of the equipment, who project themselves far out in front in technical development and thereby improve their competitiveness.'

TCO, November 1999

---

[3] 'The TCO enviro-labelling in IT — a case study of demand shaping and union proactivity', Dr Tech Ernst Hollander, Economic Institute of University College of Gaevle.

> 'Nokia became market leader in Sweden when we TCO-labelled our displays. Sales have rocketed and the growth is mostly due to the TCO labelling scheme'
>
> Anders Larsson, Business Development Manager, Northern Europe, Nokia Display Products. Interview March 2000

Suppliers' experience

A key person within the Swedish division of Nokia has been interviewed. From the very beginning Nokia has been engaged in developing displays meeting the standards set by TCO. In the late 1980s, after development work, that took less than one year, Nokia had displays that could match the considered standards. Since then, Nokia has been an active partner for TCO when discussing if considered requirements are technologically feasible. It is important to stress that the TCO requirements are well known by Nokia's designers and product developers. The requirements are part of the specifications that should be met when developing new products. It is not a question of making adaptation in a new developed product until it reaches the TCO requirements. Relevant subsuppliers are forced to deliver intermediates that cause no conflicts fulfilling the TCO requirements.

Nokia has become market leader in Sweden since they have TCO labelled their displays. The interviewed persons insist that the growth is mostly due to the TCO labelling scheme.

All displays from Nokia are TCO-certified and Nokia uses the TCO label proactive in their marketing. The label is depicted in advertisements for Nokia and information about the TCO labelling scheme is available at Nokia's home page http://www.nokia.se. When a new display is introduced on the market Nokia sends out a press release stressing that the display is TCO-certified. The parameters where the product is better than the TCO requirements are highlighted. Nokia uses the information material prepared by TCO when informing their customers in more detail about which criteria is met when a product is TCO labelled. Furthermore, as a follow-up step, Nokia has marketing specialists visiting school classes informing about how to adjust the displays.

Additionally, questionnaires were sent out to other IT manufacturers. One of these directed our attention to a self-declaration developed by the organisation of Swedish IT companies in 1996. Some manufactures prefer to use this self-declaration, in their marketing. The declaration requires no third party testing and gives space for more specific information about performance than a label. These are the main reasons for preferring the self-declaration instead of, or in addition to the TCO label. More information about the declaration can be found at www.sito.se.

3.2.5. Impression of effectiveness and scale of application

> 'Had the testing been mandatory the standards to be met by the visual display units tested, might have been set at such a low level that they wouldn't have been technology driving.'
>
> Dr Ernst Hollander. January 1999.

It is the impression that the TCO labelling scheme has an important influence on the development of more OSH sound office equipment. Suppliers have met a strong market request on TCO-labelled displays and now manufacturers all over the world have realised the importance of fulfilling the TCO requirements. The influence is probably most significant when new product groups are included by the labelling scheme. However, tightening of requirements and additional requirements to product groups already covered will also result in a pressure for product development. One could assume that the technology driving effect might not have been as effective if the labelling scheme had been mandatory and if requirements should have been negotiated with more stakeholders. Keeping the label as a voluntary scheme and having one part (TCO) in charge of setting up the requirements, TCO has great latitude to act rapidly and restrictively. These circumstances together with the homogeneous and large number of members in TCO are considered to be very important factors for TCO's success in using the market forces. The existence of ambitious manufacturers and suppliers who see a market advantage in developing products fulfilling the requirements is also regarded as being very important.

Similar initiatives seem to be applicable as a motivating factor for the development of more OSH sound products if:

- manufacturers believe that fulfilling the requirements result in enlarged market shares;
- the users are concerned about the existing products;
- the users concern can be communicated in common demands, i.e. through centralised procurement of large quantities.

3.2.6. Further information

More information: Material about the TCO labelling scheme and the TCO'99 certification can be obtained from TCO Utveckling AB, Linnégatan 14, S-11494 Stockholm. Tel. (46-8) 782 91 00; fax (46-8) 782 92 07; e-mail: Development@tco.se. Additional information is also provided on TCO's home page http://www.tco.se:8888/datamil/datami_ut.htm. Additional information about how Nokia has used the TCO labelling scheme in their marketing can be obtained from Nokia Svenska AB, Attention: Mr Anders Larsson, PO Box 1113, S-16422 Kista. Tel. (46-8) 793 83 00; fax (46-8) 793 84 41

3.3 MARKETING MANAGEMENT SYSTEMS — THE 6E MANAGEMENT SCHEME

- Sweden
- Integrated OSH and environmental management system
- Small enterprises
- Voluntary certification
- Marketing tool

6E is a working model for the development of suitable workplaces devised by the Swedish TCO Development Unit. 6E includes support material, training, consultancy and IT supporting tool.

3.3.1. Background

This case study describes the voluntary 6E scheme. The scheme was introduced in 1997 by the trade union TCO (The Swedish Confederation of Professional Employees). The 6E scheme is a tool for establishing an integrated OSH and environmental management system. 6E provides a step-by-step method, offers suitable material as checklists, computer support and training materials and a knowledge network to support the entire procedure from preparing the process to obtain the third party approval and follow-up through continuous OSH and external environmental work.

Following the steps in the scheme the company can obtain a 6E certification, but the detailed guidelines and the toolbox might be useful whatever the company applies for a 6E approval or another kind of environmental approval, i.e. an ISO 14001 certificate.

The goal of the 6E scheme is to improve OSH in small and medium-sized companies without increasing the external environmental burdens. TCO has for many years worked with questions concerning improvement of the working environment. TCO considers the development of an integrated environmental system as an obvious next step. As TCO put it: 'All development in recent years has shown that environmental adaptation brings profit. Profitability reinforces companies and organisations, which in turn creates jobs'.

The purpose of 6E is to:
- provide companies with a certification they can use in their marketing;
- present a basis for decision-making before embarking on environmental work;
- provide a systematic method of starting integrated environmental work by providing practical assistance in preparation, training, implementation and follow-up the process;
- inspire companies to begin environmental work, which covers both OSH and external environmental tasks.

The model has the name '6E' because it focuses and is built on cooperation between six areas: ergonomics, economy, ecology, emissions, efficiency and energy.

Ergonomics
The working environment in general, along with the manufactured products, shall be so well designed that there is no risk to human health.

Economy
All aspects of planning, production and distribution are approached in an economical way that takes into account optimal resource utilisation to the benefit of the employees, the company and the environment.

Ecology
All production and distribution are founded on the premise that natural renewable resources shall be used as much as possible.

Emissions
All radiation and effluents that involve risks for either humans or nature shall be eliminated, or if this is not possible, minimised to an acceptable level.

Efficiency
Utilising human creativity, imagination and knowledge while employing environmentally adapted technology to develop good products via acceptable production processes.

Energy
Energy-efficient technology should be used for all production and product use. In addition the principles of recycling and reclamation must be adhered to.

The integrated 6E management system consists of tools, supporting material in the environmental work as well as in the process, i.e.:

- a working model;
- mapping out support tool;
- education and training support;
- support to the documentation part;
- support to an internal and external audits.

3.3.2. Focus on occupational safety and health

Regarding OSH, the 6E covers checklists to map the companies performance and computer support with basic facts, search tool for legislation and regulation and a guide to further reading within the following parameters.

Physical Influence Factors

- Health care
- Risks, safety
- Protection against electrical fields
- Noise
- Electrical hypersensitivity
- Strain
- Allergies, hypersensitivity
- Lighting
- Indoor Air Climate
- Office furniture
- Premises
- Cleaning

Psycho-social Influence Factors

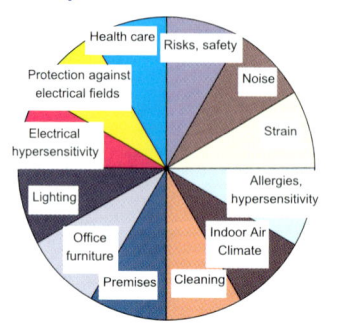

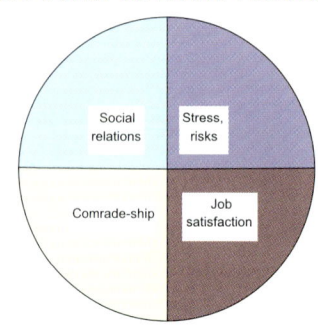

- Social relations
- Stress, risks
- Comrade-ship
- Job satisfaction

The practical working model comprises 15 steps to go through when using the checklists, computer support, the project binders and the training material. Returning to a previous step might be necessary if inconsistency shows. TNO Development acts as a sparring partner. In the following the OSH relevant actions are highlighted.

Step 1
Anchoring the work within the management. Among other things, the management discusses and clarifies which motivation forces should carry the work through. Resource allocations, i.e. staff, time and equipment should be dealt with and the relevant internal communication to ensure effective results should be planned.

Step 2
The management declares their intentions to improve OSH and the external environment and the strategic importance by establishing an environmental policy, a training plan and a project plan with milestones, personal and economic resources.

Step 3
Possibilities and obstacles are discussed.

Step 4
Anchoring the work within the organisation. Motivation factors are discussed and a common understanding is reached. Thus 6E inevitably involves change, it is vital that all employees agree with the aim and feel motivated. The practices offered by 6E stimulate a sense of togetherness at the workplace and thereby create the inner motivation factor necessary for successful environmental integration.

Step 5
The organisation and administration of the work is decided.

Step 6
Training of employees are carried out either by training of all employees or in-depth training of a lesser number who train the other employees (training of trainers approach).

Step 7
Mapping out the company's present OSH and external environmental performance.

Step 8
Documentation of the present OSH and external environmental performance. On basis of the present status, a prioritised ranking of the identified problems is established.

Step 9
The environmental policy is revised in the light of the prioritised problem areas.

Step 10
Goals are defined and measures to achieve the goals are defined.

Step 11
An action plan is prepared pointing out which goals should be reached for, which measures to be taken, when the measures should be implemented and which resources are necessary to reach the goal.

Step 12
The measures are accomplished and measures and the work process are documented.

Step 13
An audit is carried out. If the company wants a 6E certification, the audit has to be carried out by an accredited third party.

Step 14
The 6E-certification is received and the company can use the 6E label marketing the company.

Step 15
The competence is built up during the working process: planning, carrying out, follow-up.

3.3.3. Current use of the scheme

Two Swedish companies have been 6E-certified by May 2000. An additional 23 Swedish companies have for the last 3 to 4 years been working towards a certification. At present, the 6E material is only available in Swedish. However, information material about the 6E is translated into English. TCO intends to introduce the 6E scheme internationally when it has been reviewed on the basis of the experiences gained by the first 25 pilot companies.

3.3.4. Experiences

The 6E scheme was first intended for service companies and the majority of the support material currently available concerns office work. However, the working methods embodied in 6E are founded on certain basic precepts that apply to all kinds of production, whether for goods or services.

When the test-pilot audits are finished by TCO, a Swedish environmental research institute, IVF evaluates the 6E by evaluating the work carried out in 25 pilot companies.

TCO assesses that the 6E method is very useful in order to initiate the integrated environmental work. However, more specific tools should supplement the 6E when the companies reach the point where specific solutions are required to solve an OSH or an external environmental problem. Realising this, TCO considers dividing the toolbox into sections, one section dealing with physical strain, one section dealing with noise, etc. The companies should then be offered to buy only the more unfolded sections, which are of specific relevance for them. Another revision discussed is to divide the 6E tool into a number of branch-oriented sections. TCO will carry out these revisions before offering the 6E to the international market.

'6E is like a hammer. It is useful as a first tool when building something, but more tools are required if you want to finish the job'.

Anna Pramborg, TCO Development. Interview March, 2000

Purchasers' experience

There are 25 companies in the association 'Svenska Inredare', who are working as pilot companies with the 6E certificate. So far two of the companies have been certified. The reason why the companies have started this work is based on the assumption that the certificate is a good competitive parameter, and the companies gain a better position in the market, as OHS is a demand from many purchasers. The pilot companies are all small or smaller companies (4–8 employees).

As only two companies have obtained the certificate recently, the companies do not have much experience today with the 6E certificate as a sales and marketing parameter. However, one of the certified companies says in a press release that the company has improved their structure and fewer people leave the company because of the results obtained by the 6E measures. Some of the companies also mention that they have increased their market share thanks to their involvement in 6E.

The certification costs are relatively high and the management and the employees must be motivated, and the personnel have to be educated and trained. The companies have often allocated a person responsible for the environment.

The assumptions are that the cost/benefit is anticipated to be positive because working procedures will be more efficient, and the business volume will increase. TCO has informed the project team that one of the 6E companies has obtained a loan because of their 6E work.

The 6E-certified companies expect that they will be more competitive in relation to their competitors.

Suppliers' experience

TCO states that suppliers are well aware of the demands and the 6E companies cooperate with the smaller suppliers to make them meet their requirements.

However, some of the suppliers have reacted negatively on the OHS requirements, but it looks like none of the suppliers have been excluded due to non-compliance with the OHS requirements.

3.3.5. Impression of effectiveness and scale of application

The 6E-integrated management system seems to be a comprehensive system, with a well-worked-out tool kit for starting up systematic environmental and OSH work in small companies. The declaration seems to be a good motivational factor for companies and may help to drive the process forward, even when the small companies could be tempted to drop out of the implementation of the system due to pressure of business. However, the system is still very new and more experiences where the declaration has been used, as a marketing tool, need to be generated before 6E's effectiveness as a marketing tool can be evaluated.

3.3.6. Further information

More information: Material about the 6E scheme can be obtained from TCO Utveckling AB, Linnégatan 14, S-11494 Stockholm. Tel. (46-8) 782 91 00; fax (46-8) 782 92 07; e-mail: Development@tco.se. Information is also available on the home page http://www.tco-info.com/6e.html

3.4 MARKETING OF BAKERY EQUIPMENT — NF HSA BY BONGARD

- France
- Product label
- Product safety
- Safety and comfort related to the use of equipment
- Bakery industry

3.4.1 Background

The issue: Since 1922, Bongard has manufactured bread and cake-making equipment. It employs 600 people and 60 % of its products are exported throughout the world. It is the leading firm in its market in France and Europe and has a comprehensive range of products. Safety, in all its forms, is a concern in this firm for both its personnel and its products. Its customer base is very broad, ranging from the local artisan to the supermarket and the multinational retail chain. The feature of its catalogue is that it contains products with a long life which are manufactured in small runs virtually on demand. It should be noted that Bongard operates in a field in which the regulations have changed greatly due to European legislation. But Bongard's business places the firm in a field in which self-certification of machines is the rule (its products are not listed in Appendix IV to the 98/37/EC 'Machinery' directive where machines considered particularly dangerous are listed and covered by a third-party certification procedure).

Objective: Bongard has developed numerous technical innovations designed to improve the reliability and ease of use of its products. Great importance is assigned to human engineering. All the products in the catalogue scrupulously comply with the essential safety and health procedures and requirements of the 98/37/EC 'Machinery' directive. But Bongard has endeavoured to go further in developing products which give satisfaction to the user of the machine (comfort, fitness for purpose) and which ensure the best possible hygiene for the consumer.

Means: Bongard intends to be responsive to all the repercussions of legislative changes on its market. Bongard's aim is to help its industry and its market to keep up with the changes in European legislation. This translates into strong involvement in standardisation work at the European and French levels and effective follow-up of customers. Given its position as leader, Bongard has pressed for the organisation of a manufacturers' trade association and the introduction of a label specific to the industry.

3.4.2. Focus on occupational safety and health

Bongard constantly seeks greater safety, as this is one of the fundamental aspects of its corporate culture.

For Bongard the only good commercial policy is to manufacture reliable, easy-to-maintain and safe products. When the 'Machinery' directive was implemented, its products did not have to be changed because they were already in conformity with the new directive. The only adaptations were confined to re-editing of the technical manuals. Asbestos was removed from all products in 1988. Thinking is currently in progress on ceramics with a view to replacing this substitute for asbestos, which does not seem to meet the required safety criteria. Great attention is paid to the elimination of flour dust given off by kneading machines and beaters.

When the 'Machinery' directive and the directive on 'Establishment of equipment conformance' were transcribed into French law, Bongard helped promote awareness in its industry and among its customers through information campaigns carried out jointly with the Machines and Alimentary Products Tests Laboratory (Laboratoire d'Essais des Matériels et Produits Alimentaires — LEMPA) and the Bakery and Pastry French Producers Union (Union des Fabricants Français d'Équipements pour la Boulangerie et la Pâtisserie — UFFEB). This action took the form of publication of the 'Safety guide in bread and cake baking'.

There is constant communication on product safety targeted at the dealers. All the installed products can be easily located and monitored thanks to a specific database. The upgrades made necessary by the new requirements and technical progress are covered by technical data sheets, which are sent out to the dealers. Upgrading kits are developed for the machines in question. This was especially the case for bringing into conformity machines dating prior to 1980. If customers dismount the safety devices, the after sales department must put them back again and notify these problems in a written report to the parent company. All equipment, which returns to the factory without protective devices, is sent back to the customer equipped with those protective devices.

3.4.3. Current use of application of the scheme

Bongard's involvement in the NF HSA label's development:

To ensure the overall safety of the equipment used in bread and cake-baking, Bongard has acted so that its industry became organised to facilitate the setting up of its own inspection agency. This procedure materialised in the creation of a technical secretariat specific to the bread and cake-baking equipment manufacturing industry. This technical secretariat, with the evocative name of

'Group for the Improvement of Equipment designed for Institutional Catering' operates as a subcontractor to AFNOR for the certification of machinery. This enabled the introduction of a label more specific to the bread making industry: NF HSA.

> *The quest for quality meant to go beyond the legislative requirements.*

NF HSA is an acronym for the French words meaning French standards, H for food hygiene, S for safety and A for fitness for purpose. This label goes beyond the hygiene and safety requirements of the 'Machinery' directive because it also deals with ease of cleaning and certifies that the equipment is indeed destined for the originally planned use.

This labelling is a voluntary procedure. There is a cost involved in obtaining the NF HSA label, especially since this operation is performed on short runs. The manufacturing process is also inspected because the continuity of production quality must be ensured.

Functioning: Technical specifications define the requirements to obtain or retain the NF HSA brand. There are specific technical specifications for each type of machine. With regard to hygiene and safety, this document refers to all the European standards and adds to this the concept of fitness for purpose. This concerns both the design and manufacture of the product. It is the Machines and alimentary products tests laboratory (LEMPA) which is responsible for the laboratory tests. Depending on the result of these tests, the NF HSA labelling committee (consisting of prevention organisations, manufacturers and users) may or may not decide to award the label which is issued by AFNOR.

3.4.4. Experiences

Originality: The NF HSA label is a voluntary certification procedure, which testifies to the quality, safety and reliability of the product. It aims, therefore, to reinforce customers' confidence in these products. Another benefit is that it marks Bongard's products and the other labelled products off from the competition. Compliance with safety and quality rules thus becomes a sales argument.

> *'Bongard is a company forging ahead in terms of safety and health'.*
>
> Mr Hardouin — Panifour's General Manager

Experience of buyers: Bongard distributes its products via a worldwide network of dealers. This network is stable, its members are signatories of a quality charter and are trained by the firm. If the products' price is above the market average their quality is proportional to the price. While the end customer is increasingly sensitive to safety and health matters, he still keeps a close watch on the cost of acquisitions. Integrating safety into the whole enables them to contribute actively to overall product quality which is best accepted by the customers. These products are covered by a contractual warranty ranging from 5 to 10 years on certain components. Many large accounts work with Bongard, especially hypermarket company Carrefour which has chosen it for its establishments in Asia. Panifour, a major dealer for France, indicated the plus offered by Bongard products by giving a definite comfort of use. This company, concerned with safety and health, has a very well-equipped engineering office, which places it at the front of its field. For this distributor, the major strengths of Bongard are certification and the NF HSA label. Bongard, moreover, does not hesitate to insist on its strict compliance with prevailing hygiene and safety standards in its sales brochures.

Relations with suppliers: These relations are based on principles of partnership and loyalty. In practice, the purchasing policy places strong emphasis on the safety of products and components. All components and parts incorporated in the finished products are bought for their intrinsic safety and health qualities in either the manufacture of the product itself or in its use. Each product or component proposed must be accompanied by its technical data sheet, which must include a section on safety. The occupational physician is asked to validate the choices made. If validation is not granted, the search begins for a substitute. If two products are available at the same price, the safest one will be chosen.

3.4.5. Impression of effectiveness and scale of application

Through its position as leader in this market, Bongard demonstrates that a more stringent approach is possible. The integration of safety in all forms (safety for the worker and food safety for the consumer) into an overall quality procedure is appreciated by customers so long as the extra cost remains reasonable.

3.4.6. Further information

Mr Axel Leterreux, Bongard, 32, route de Wolfisheim, F-67810 Holtzheim. Tel. (33) 388 78 00 23; fax (33) 388 76 19 18; e-mail: axelleterreux@bongard.fr

4.

GOVERNMENTAL MARKETING INITIATIVES

4.1 STIMULATING OSH MARKETING — THE DANISH WORKING ENVIRONMENT LABEL

- Denmark
- Considered for implementation
- Marketing tool
- Attracting of employees

The Danish Ministry of Labour

- A Danish Working Environment Label

4.1.1. Background

This case study describes a feasibility study identifying the possibilities and obstacles for establishing a voluntary Danish working environment label. The label has not been introduced yet, but may become a reality in Denmark from the year 2001. A pilot project is planned and, on the back of this, it will be decided politically whether the label should be introduced or not.

In 1998 a political framework agreement between the Danish Ministry of Labour and the Danish Socialist People's Party was established. OSH prevention should be prioritised and new tools for OSH work developed. Based on the agreement, a number of activities were initiated, and a working environment label was pointed out as a priority area.

The scheme is called 'working environmental label'. However, it is planned to be a label assigned to companies with an outstanding OSH performance. A more appropriate name for the scheme would therefore be 'working environment certificate'.

The working environment label is intended to be a governmental initiative encouraging companies to improve their OSH.

The purpose is to provide companies with good working conditions with a marketing tool — the working environment label — and hereby make OSH a competitive parameter.

> Companies certified with the label are expected to gain advantages with regards to:
> - attracting and keeping employees;
> - expanding sales of their products, goods and/or services;
> - maintaining or obtaining a good reputation in society, i.e. among investors, politicians and organisations.

The requirements of the working environment label have been discussed with different stakeholders. The discussion has focused on whether the requirements should be identical for all business sectors or not.

The following arguments have been highlighted for and against sector-specific requirements.

In favour of specific requirements: The OSH situation differs within the different branches and different OSH problems are in focus. Branch-specific requirements would then reflect those OSH problems, which in general are the most predominant for the specific branch.

Against specific requirements: It will be more time consuming to establish and revise the scheme as well as to identify and specify relevant requirements for all the different sectors. In addition, the administration will be more time consuming if sector specific requirements are used, as it will require administration of a number of more or less different schemes. If more business sectors compete for the same qualifications and if the requirements vary from sector to sector it may result in competitive disadvantage. Furthermore, it has been discussed whether the working environment label should be a separate scheme or if the requirements should be implemented in an existing scheme, i.e. a voluntary supplement to the environmental requirements defined in the Danish scheme 'Green accounting'. The following arguments have been stressed for and against establishing the working environment label as a separate scheme.

The feasibility study was carried out from December 1998 to June 1999 with the purpose of establishing a solid basis for further discussions about the general interest in the labelling scheme and possible incentives.

The Danish Working Environment Service

Memorandum on a voluntary Danish scheme for a working environment label

Contents

1	**Introduction**
2	**The most important variables in a scheme**
2.1	Company- or product-oriented scheme
2.2	Sector-oriented or non-sector-oriented scheme
2.3	The actual working environment or initiatives taken in the working environment
2.4	Extension of the working environment concept
2.5	How many criteria, and how restrictive
2.6	Independent or integrated scheme
2.7	Label or working environment declaration
3	**Administration**
4	**Empirical testing**

In favour of a separate scheme: A label focusing separately on OSH will provide a clearer signal compared to a situation where OSH is just one element among others to be fulfilled. If the label is established as a separate scheme, it will be independent of existing formats and it will be possible to establish immediately.

Against a separate scheme: The stakeholders are not familiar with the working environment label and a massive marketing of the scheme is necessary to inform about the scheme and to build up its credibility. Another argument relates to the introduction of a new scheme among many other existing schemes, which might be considered a burden on the companies.

4.1.2. Focus on occupational safety and health

All requirements will go beyond what is required by the OSH legislation, meaning that only companies fulfilling the legal requirements can apply and obtain the working environment label. The working environment label will focus on probably all of the following aspects:

- the actual OSH level;
- the OSH initiatives;
- other OSH-related factors.

OSH level

Requirements focusing on the actual OSH level will reward companies for a specific good OSH standard. Focus will be on obtained results and not only on good intentions.

OSH initiatives

Requirements focusing on the OSH work provide a possibility to reward the companies for their efforts to obtain a good OSH standard. Both OSH management systems and environmental management systems are focusing on the process towards specific goals. If focus for the working environment label is put on the process instead of the obtained results, the working environment label could be supported by well-known procedures, e.g. as laid down in the Danish regulation on workplace assessment (APV) in EMAS or ISO 14001. The OSH goals could be part of the company's environmental policy. Control and auditing of OSH could be carried out as part of audits on already implemented management systems.

A broader OSH context

Requirements regarding other social aspects influencing the working environment have been discussed, such as training/education, alcohol policies and smoking policies and other issues relevant for the broader term 'working condition'.

4.1.3. Current use of the scheme

The Danish working environment label has not been implemented yet. A pilot project is planned to take place in the beginning of year 2001. The results should provide a basis for a label, which may be introduced in Denmark in year 2001.

4.1.4. Experiences

As the working environment label is not yet implemented, there are no experiences with a possible impact. However, the feasibility study indicates the potential market response.

Research interviews have been carried out with OSH experts and PR and marketing experts. They explain how they believe the market will react on a working environment label. The respondents find that the idea of certifying companies based on OSH parameters sounds reasonable. Several of the interviewed persons think that a working environment label will generate a positive image of the certified companies. The respondents also believe that a label will result in a positive effect regarding recruiting and keeping employees. However, the respondents do not believe a label will affect the individual consumer and then the label does not necessarily offer any specific personal advantages for the consumers. In addition, the respondents stress that a working environment label might result in undesirable effects, if — for instance — companies primarily perform their OSH work to fulfil requirements directed by the working environment label, when other OSH problems are in fact more urgent. Also the influence of the employees on the ranking of which problems are the more important than others may be reduced.

Several of the interviewed persons stress the importance of having requirements covering both the physical and the psychological aspects of OSH as both aspects are very important for how the employee experience their working conditions. Furthermore, it is stressed that the conception of OSH is not static. Issues included in the conception of OSH have changed over time. According to the respondents, employees find especially that psychological and social issues are important for their conception of a good working life, whereas these issues are partly delimited from the official conception of OSH. If a working environment label only includes requirements regarding the physical OSH, the label will be in direct contravention to the employees understanding of which elements should be evaluated and accepted before the OSH should be rewarded.

Purchasers' experience

The target groups, expected to pay specific attention to the label include professional purchasers. But other stakeholder groups can also be understood as 'purchaser' of the message delivered by the label. Most important are probably the employees and potential new employees. Additionally, the investors may be a relevant target group.

Based on interviews with representatives from the above-mentioned groups, the feasibility study has indicated how the 'purchasers' are expected to react to a working environment label. The interviews were carried out among stakeholders from two different branches, slaughterhouses and cleaning services. A total of 40 stakeholders were interviewed.

To qualify the interviews, two proposals (dummies) for a working environment label were developed, — one exemplifying a sector oriented working environment label, including sector-specific requirements and the other exemplifying a non-sector oriented working environment label, including requirements relevant for all sectors. The dummies were sent out to the respondents before the interviews to make sure that the respondents have the same idea of what was meant by a working environment label.

'There is a need for something that can give a company a possibility to show if they are doing something extraordinary. Here a working environment label could be a good idea.'

Employee within the slaughterhouse branch, April 1999

Employees

In general, the employees in the slaughterhouses show great interest in a working environment label. The employees expect that the label may act as a lever to improve OSH within their branch. The employees find that a voluntary scheme would be appropriate and expect that companies with good performance will apply for the label. However, the employees believe that the business should be focusing more on OSH before the label will obtain a notable effect. The employees within the cleaning service found that in general a working environment label would be reasonable. However, the label will not necessarily affect the employees' choice of working place, because employees within the cleaning sector very often work part time and choose their workplace depending on salary and geographical position.

Professional purchasers

The purchasers reply that a working environment label will have little impact on which companies are chosen to deliver goods or services. For the retailers purchasing meat, a working environment label will be of less interest because the label is expected to have no influence on the private consumers. Private consumers are expected to have interest in OSH only in relation to working conditions for employees in the third world. However, an issue as employee turnover might be in focus when purchasing services, i.e. cleaning, and a working environmental label could be given priority. The purchasers point out that a working environmental label might be mentioned as a pre-qualification requirement when inviting tenders.

Investors

'The products should not be too expensive. Welfare and employee arrangements could easily be thought out. It costs, but on the other side a good OSH climate, employee satisfaction and stability are also important for the production. Ten crowns spent on employee satisfaction is 10 crowns taken from the profit — the money for the shareholders. But the money can be well spent. It is important to find the right balance.'

Investor, April 1999

The interviewed investors reply that in general they pay little attention to OSH. Only if the OSH performance differs considerably from the average level, OSH obtains specific interest from the investors.

Suppliers' experience

The suppliers' interest for a working environment label is related to the interest among management representatives to have their companies certified according to a working environment label. The management representatives from the slaughterhouses are reluctant to implement a working environment label, whereas the management representatives from the cleaning services are more positive. However, both groups are of the opinion that a label will only have little effect regarding the possibilities of these specific sectors to attract and keep employees. Within other business sectors the effect might be more significant.

4.1.5. Impression of effectiveness and scale of application

The effect of a working environment label depends on the interest within the market. The primary driving force for a working environment label is considered to be the employees. If employees should value the label and prefer a job within a certified company, the requirements for obtaining the label should cover social aspects as well as psychological and physical aspects. Social aspects are for example flexible working schedules, senior employee policies, possibilities for training and education, possibilities for working at home and company kinder gardens.

In Denmark, the number of qualified employees are limited within certain business sectors and in certain geographical areas. Within those sectors and areas, the project team believes that a working environment label could be one of the factors guiding the employees, assuming that the label reflects the company's social, psychological and physical OSH performance.

The professional purchaser could also be an important stakeholder for a working environment label. When professional purchasers procure services they or their customers are in direct contact with the contractors' staff. In these cases, the importance of the working conditions of the contractors is most obviously of interest for the purchaser as well. Some public purchasers have pointed out that a working environment label could be used as a pre-qualification when inviting tenders. If public purchasers do so, the working environment label will be a strong marketing tool.

A working environment label is assessed to be most applicable within the following business sectors:

- sectors having difficulties in attracting qualified employees;
- sectors carrying out services procured by professional purchasers.

4.1.6. Further information

Further information about the Danish initiative can be obtained from the Danish Ministry of Labour, Division 3, Tel. (45) 33 92 59 00 or by the National Working Environment Authority, Head of Division 1, Peter Herskind. Tel. (45) 39 15 20 00

COWI, Consulting Engineers and Planners, which has carried out the feasibility study, would also be pleased to assist with more information. Tel. (45) 45 97 22 11. Contact persons will be Mr Torben Bruun Hansen, TBH@COWI.DK or Ms. Marchen Vinding Petersen MVP@COWI.DK

European Agency for Safety and Health at Work

SYSTEMS AND PROGRAMMES

5.

OSH IN PROCUREMENT AT COMPANY LEVEL

5.1 PROCUREMENT IN THE CONSTRUCTION SECTOR — THE DANISH LANDWORKS, ØRESUND FIXED LINK

- Denmark
- Large construction work
- Requirements for contractors
- Site inspections and audits
- OSH campaigns

5.1.1. Background

This case study describes a number of initiatives taken in order to reduce occupational accidents at the large construction project, the Øresund fixed link between Denmark and Sweden. The initiative to reduce occupational accidents was, among other things, based on the experiences gained while building the Danish fixed link across the Great Belt. Many accidents occurred during this construction work and a political will to do better when building the Øresund link was pronounced.

The link includes a four-lane motorway and a dual-track railway linking Copenhagen and Malmö. The construction work consists of three elements:

1. The Danish landworks. Client: A/S Øresund

The Danish landworks, consists of an 18 km, dual-track railway with stations in Ørestaden, Tårnby and Copenhagen Airport in Kastrup and a 9 km four-lane motorway between the existing traffic system and Copenhagen Airport and on to the coast-to-coast facility.

2. The fixed coast-to-coast link. Client: Øresundskonsortiet

The coast-to-coast link comprises a four-lane motorway and a dual-track electrified railway between Lernacken on the Swedish side and Kastrup on the Danish side. In total, the link is almost 16 km long and passes an artificial peninsula off the Danish coast, a 3.5 km tunnel, an artificial island about 4 km long and a 7.8 km bridge composed of a two-level high bridge and two approach bridges.

3. The Swedish landworks. Client: Svedab

The Swedish landworks include a 10 km long stretch of motorway and railway from Lernacken to Lockarp/Fosieby, upgrading of the existing continental line railway, and upgrading of Malmö freight terminal. In addition, the Swedish Vägverket is building a 10 km motorway to connect to E6 north of Malmö.

A/S Øresund began the construction of the Danish landworks for the Øresund fixed link in September 1993. The bridge was inaugurated on the 1 July 2000.

The three building owners did not have the same business organisation and therefore used different methods when inviting tenderers. A/S Øresund and Svedab divided the work into smaller contracts and were working with many different contractors. This model implied that A/S Øresund, as building owner on the Danish side, took responsibility for incorporating OSH already when designing the works. In Denmark it is the responsibility of the building designer to incorporate OSH in the design phase. Additionally, A/S Øresund and Svedab had a responsibility to coordinate the safety issues, i.e. when more contractors were working in the same area.

This case study describes how the Danish building owner A/S Øresund has:
- set up OSH and environmental requirements when inviting tenderers;
- established an organisation to follow up and carry out auditing;
- initiated a campaign in cooperation with the two other clients.

> For A/S Øresund the objective of starting OSH initiatives were:
> - to reduce the number of occupational accidents by 50 % compared to the average within the building industry;
> - to obtain a good reputation by communicating that 'any accident is one too many'.

A/S Øresund had an environmental policy, which in relation to OSH, stated that maximum attention should be paid to the employees' safety and health, both when planning and carrying out the work. Additionally, it was stated that the work should be planned and carried out so that no worker was exposed to any risk. Right from the start, this policy was the measure for success for the building owner.

A/S Øresund established an OSH and environmental staff function with reference directly to the managing director of A/S Øresund. Four full-time persons were employed to implement the OSH and environmental policy of A/S Øresund. Approximately, one and a half full-time employees were allocated specifically to OSH issues and were involved in:
- setting up OSH and environmental requirements in tender material for contractors;
- evaluating the planners templates for safety and health plans;
- evaluating contractors' tenders;
- taking action related to input from site inspections and audits;
- acting as A/S Øresund's representative in the OSH campaigns;
- evaluating the obtained results.

Furthermore, four full-time employees were employed primarily to carry out OSH site inspections, lead the regular safety meetings held in areas where more contractors were working at the same time, and in general guide the contractors in OSH-related questions. Finally, independent consultants certified as OSH auditors were employed to carry out OSH audits.

Before starting the work, A/S Øresund was certified according to ISO 9001, ISO 14001 (draft version) and in 1997 also according to BS 8800.

A/S Øresund did not require tenderers to be ISO-certified, because it would have limited the number of contractors able to make an offer too much. Instead A/S Øresund defined a number of requirements and an independent consulting firm evaluated the contractors' bids. The parameters evaluated included the performance with respect to price, OSH, quality and environment.

5.1.2. Focus on occupational safety and health

'The main focus has been on the prevention of occupational accidents. A number of instruments have been applied in order to prevent accidents:

OSH and environmental requirements in tender materials

In the tender material, the contractors were asked to make a plan for safety and health. This requirement gave A/S Øresund a possibility to evaluate the contractors' attitude to OSH. From mid-1994 the tender material included a template for a safety and health plan in which the contractors should add information about the methods and equipment they intended to use and the possible impact on human health. Information on the expected need for personal protective equipment should also be included. Various planners completed the templates based on information about the specific contract. If A/S Øresund found a template incomplete, because it did not cover all work-related risks, the template was returned to the planners for improvement.

Having received the contractors' offers, A/S Øresund asked an independent consulting firm to evaluate the proposals. Depending on the nature of the contracted work and the related human risk, OSH counted for approximately

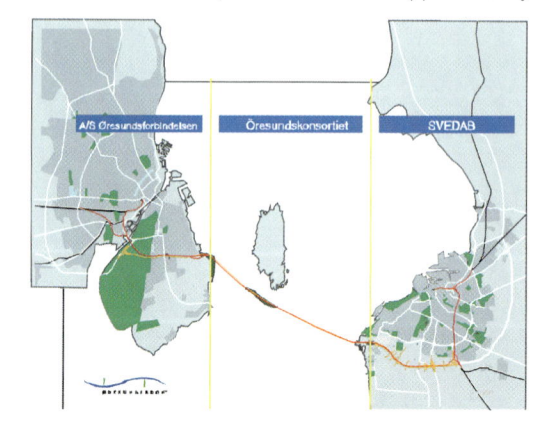

When the constructor takes safety seriously, the contractor takes safety seriously and then the management takes safety seriously and the employees take safety seriously.'

Jørgen Huno Rasmussen, Adm. Director, H. Hoffmann & Sønner A/S, Denmark. Statement in the Danish report 'Godt begyndt — halvt fuldent', October 1995 to June 1997

5–15 % among other issues when the consulting firm recommended which contractor A/S Øresund should choose.

Follow up and auditing

Immediately after a contractor had been chosen and before the work began an introduction meeting was held. At this meeting, A/S Øresund stressed the requirements related to the plan for safety and health and the contractor presented the guidelines for structuring his work. While the contracted work was ongoing, A/S Øresund carried out audits to ensure that the contractor implemented and reviewed his plan for safety and health. In general, the audit frequency was 1 to 2 times per year. Audits were carried out as a coordinated action combining quality, environment and OSH auditing by having auditors representing all three kinds of skills visiting the same workplace at the same time. The auditors were certified as OSH auditors according to the Danish auditor programme established by DIEU, Danish International Continuing Education.

Furthermore, A/S Øresund had four OSH coordinators employed full-time to carry out inspections and advice the contractors in OSH questions. The OSH coordinators were authorised to stop work, which was not considered safe and in compliance with previously received information from the contractor. This was a measure which had actually been brought into play a couple of times during the project period. The contractors were obliged to participate in the audits and the inspections with a number of requested persons. Also subcontractors could be subject to an audit, although it was the main contractors who were responsible for passing on the requirements to the subcontractors and making sure that only subcontractors fulfilling A/S Øresund's requirements were used.

Notification of accidents was another instrument in use. All contractors were requested to report all occupational accidents to A/S Øresund. Both accidents which were legally requested to be reported to the Danish Working Environment Authority (accidents which result in one or more days of absence in addition to the day the accident occurred) and near misses should be reported. The notification procedure was used to follow up on occupational accidents and was considered very useful in the dialog with contractors.

OSH campaign

In order to motivate contractors to prevent accidents and improve OSH, an OSH campaign was established in 1995 in a cooperation between the three building owners. A mascot — a beaver — was introduced to create identity and team spirit. The mascot was placed on huge posters at the entrance to the construction sites bearing the text, 'We take care here'. Some contractors also awarded a mascot to employees who had completed an obligatory safety-training course. By wearing the mascot-label on the helmet the employee showed that he or she was ready to start working for the contractor.

An OSH prize of approximately EUR 3 600 was awarded twice a year to the contractor who put most effort in safety on the construction site. The four OSH coordinators evaluated the contractors using a scoring system when they inspected the contractors' work. The evaluation included the OSH attitude, equipment, planning, training and specific initiatives taken to improve OSH.

Actual slips and defects resulting in minus points and injunctions or bans from the Danish Working Environment Authority excluded the contractor from being nominated. The managing director of A/S Øresund then proclaimed a winner among the nominated coordinators and OSH staff.

Furthermore, a newspaper was published four times a year. The newspaper provided information on the project's progress, the OSH work and the ongoing events at A/S Øresund's different construction sites. The newspaper was distributed to all employees. The blue-collar workers received the newspaper on the site and for other employees the newspaper was available in the canteen, the reception or distributed by internal post. The newspaper was translated into Danish, Swedish and English.

In addition the campaign included a video, which could be used free of charge by the contractors and which was used as an element in the safety training courses. The video was available in Danish, Swedish and English.

Finally, bulletin boards were placed on the on-site containers and were used to inform about OSH, the campaign and warnings about specific risks, i.e. information about situations nearly resulting in accidents.

5.1.3. Current use of the scheme

The initiatives taken by A/S Øresund were to a certain extent continued in the contracted work related to the coast-to-coast project. The experience obtained from being a proactive constructor setting up OSH requirements for the contractors will most likely be continued in other public construction work in Denmark. The Danish Minister of Labour has recently proclaimed that he and the Danish Ministry of Housing discuss how the Danish State may take action being largest constructor in Denmark. The two ministers will coordinate initiatives with the purpose of setting up OSH requirements for contractors. Future contractors may be obligated to show a good OSH performance if the contractor wants to carry out contracted work for the Danish State.

5.1.4. Experiences

A/S Øresund has together with the two other constructors evaluated the effect of their OSH initiatives. The evaluations are based on questionnaires and interviews with a large number of stakeholders plus statistical surveys of occupational accidents and the causes of those accidents. Five hundred employees have received the questionnaire, 19 contractor firms and nine professional and industrial bodies have been interviewed. Additionally, the relevant authorities have stated their opinion about the effectiveness of the OSH initiatives.

The main conclusion is that the initiatives have had a substantial impact on safety and health. The employees, the contractors, the authorities and the professional and industrial bodies all have sympathy for the clear goals and the building owners' continued efforts to reach these goals.

The personal commitment shown by the management of the constructors is stressed as being crucial to the success. Establishing a team spirit and setting a common goal for reducing the number of accidents are emphasised as the most important reasons for having success.

The evaluation reveals that every third employee has gained OSH knowledge and changed their working habits during the project period. Improvements included better planning, better tidying up at the workplace, more meetings about safety and more cooperation and a feeling of better safety on the construction sites, more frequent use of personal protection equipment and more information and training in safety questions.

Purchasers' experience

In general, the goal of reducing the number of occupational accidents by 50 per cent was not completely reached. The number of accidents was reduced to 30 per one million working hours compared to a branch average of 40 per one million working hours. In spite of this, the two OSH staff employed assess that the OSH initiatives have been a success. It is however, important to note that all of the accidents that occurred during the Øresund project were reported, whereas an underreporting of accidents is typical for the branch. It should also be mentioned that four fatal accidents occurred: one while building the Danish landworks and three while building the fixed coast to coast link. Although other major projects similar to this one do not reach better safety results, fatal accidents still affect the impression of the success of the project. In this way the objective mentioned in the beginning that "any accident is one to many" is also applicable here.

Having coordinated requirements in different standards saves the contractors from difficulties in finding out which requirements to fulfil and by coordinating OSH, environmental and quality audits, and the contractors save time at the audits. The reporting and analysing of near misses have been very useful. Some persons stress that the initiative might have been even better if more information were given about how to define a near miss and if an average group had been established to analyse and take action when occupational accidents or near misses occurred.

The staff employees working with OSH explained that a few contractors gave up before tendering, but in general the contractors showed a positive attitude when

---

'When a constructor sets up (OSH) requirements something happens. All governmental and local authorities ought to do so as constructors or clients.'

Bjarne Rundberg, Team Manager, Building and Civil Works, SID, Denmark. Statement in the Danish report 'Godt begyndt — halvt fuldent', October 1995 to June 1997

'The contractor has an economic interest in working with safety issues because it is the contractor who has to pay for the first month of absence and also has a great responsibility in restoring the injured employee.'

Jan Gabrielson, Regional Manager, NCC Anläggning, Sweden. In the Danish report 'Godt begyndt — halvt fuldent', October 1995 to June 1997

met with OSH requirements. And from the constructors' point of view it was not a disadvantage to sort out the 'bad' contractors before having them on the project.

Contractors' experience

Half of the contractors' employees replied that the health and safety measures were better on the Øresund fixed link than on other construction sites.

Both the contractors and the contractors' employees considered the OSH campaign to be a positive initiative. As an example, the newspaper was read by 49 % of all employees and 49 % of the employees found that the OSH price was a good or very good initiative.

5.1.5. Impression of effectiveness and scale of application

The initiatives taken by A/S Øresund seem to have been successful, as indicated by the more limited number of occupational accidents that occurred.

The organisation built up to carry out A/S Øresund's OSH policy proved successful and in particular the commitment from the top management was important for this success. Even though the initiatives were carried out in relation to a large project and therefore may be of specific interest for big contractors, many of the methods used can be applied in relation to smaller contracts.

5.1.6. Further Information

More information regarding the Øresund link initiatives is presented in the Danish mid-term report 'Godt begyndt — halvt fuldendt' ('Well begun — half done') describing the OSH initiatives in relation to the construction project from 1997, and on the home page for the Øresund consortium (www.oresundskonsortiet.com).

'It is positive to have a constructor, who explicitly informs that this is the way he wants it to be. It works. It is the first time it is carried out with this effect in this way.'

Axel Kjær, Production Manager on shore, Højgaard & Schultz A/S, Denmark In the Danish report 'Godt begyndt — halvt fuldent', October 1995 to June 1997

5.2 PROCUREMENT IN AN INDUSTRIAL PLANT — RENAULT TECHNOCENTER

- France
- Management system — Purchasing
- Customer driven
- Management of risk factors by all the players
- Total safety procedure

5.2.1. Background

The issue: In the beginning of the 1990s, Renault planned the construction of its new technology complex. This construction project involved bringing together on a single site all the skills, from product/process design to validation, necessary to bring future vehicles to market. Renault wanted this construction site to be exemplary in terms of overall quality and occupational safety. Renault's advertising theme at the time was 'Véhicule à vivre' (cars for living), and this very same theme was adopted as the motto to be applied on the huge construction site which was then called 'Site for living'. This translated into the establishment of a safety assurance system integrated into a master plan for quality.

This ambitious project, which would last several years — from 1991 to 1993 for the preparations of the groundwork's and from 1994 to 1998 for the erection of the buildings. It covered 12 buildings representing 350 000 m² of floor space to be set up on an area of 150 hectares. This site represented 9 million hours of work distributed between 900 contractors and 10 000 persons. The size of the site risked aggravating the difficulties traditionally faced in the construction sector, namely extensive use of subcontracting, with a very large number of small and medium-sized enterprises, extensive use of temporary workers, illegal workers and low-skilled labour.

Objective: Renault management wanted to ensure that a total safety and quality policy established and applied, having learnt of the accident frequency and severity rates commonly found in the building sector and far higher than the company's own rates. Renault would not accept such rates on a site where they were the sole client.

> **Key points:**
> - efficient, centralised organisation of the site with a focus on enhanced safety;
> - owner playing a role through numerous safety initiatives;
> - strong partnership established with the prevention institutions.

Means: Renault laid down its conditions for the potential contractors. The total cost of this policy (excluding first aid post and reception costs) for Renault was FRF 18 million. This investment in safety was one facet of the search for total quality through good site management.

'The construction site showed the coordination judiciousness for the safety of the numerous workers present on the site.'

Mr F. Villa — Cramif [4] Occupational Safety Officer

Renault anticipated the coordination rule because, at that time, there was no legislation and no experience with the integration of safety in the design and execution phases. All this was prior to the 1992 directive on 'Mobile and temporary work sites' transcribed into French law in December 1994 by the decree on safety and health coordination of work sites.

There was no action taken to integrate safety into the design phase as this phase was too advanced when this system was brought into practice. On the other hand, during the execution phase, coordination was established although there was no legal obligation to do so at the start of site work, and then under the regime of the new decree. As the new directive was transcribed into French law in the middle of the project period only the last two buildings were built (started at the end of 1997) completely under the new regulations.

5.2.2. Focus on occupational safety and health

Criteria: Renault did not want its company image to be tarnished by poor occupational safety results. Moreover, it had been calculated at the start of the project that if the traditional rates in the construction industry were confirmed, the cost of non-safety would amount to around FRF 100 million, distributed among all the contractors present on the site.

Parameters: Renault fixed the following factors as parameters of success:
- improvement in the quality of life of the personnel on the site;
- no fatal accident;
- an accident frequency ([5]) of, with work stoppage, 15 or under, compared to 70 at the time in the construction industry;

([4]) Cramif — Caisse Régionale d'Assurance Maladie — Île-de-France — Paris Regional Insurance Funds.
([5]) Number of accidents with absence per million of working hours.

- a severity rate (⁶) not to exceed 0.60 compared to 3 at the time in the construction industry.

These quantifiable objectives set frequency and severity rates on average five times lower than those in the building industry. The frequency rate was also used as one of the indicators for monitoring the contractors' safety performance.

5.2.3. Current use of the system

Description of the system: To obtain these results, the involvement of all the players was essential. Renault wrote a safety policy statement according to which it committed itself to do everything in its power to ensure that the commitments made might materialise. Renault requested the contractors involved to subscribe to this policy in writing. The application of this policy required a specific system.

<u>The prevention unit</u>

This unit — coordinated by a Renault employee work condition engineer — formed the core of the system (⁷). It met once a week. All parties involved took part such as: the coordinators of the various sites, the occupational physician, the prevention officers, the logistics manager and the representatives of safety and health institutions (Labour Inspectorate, CRAM, OPPBTP). It was to become the hub for all site safety action. The permanent nature of this unit generated strong synergy between the client and all the safety players.

> 'The concern of the member of the prevention unit was to be efficient safety at work actors.'
>
> Mr S. Desgranges — Renault's Work Condition and Safety Engineer

The unit performed selection and monitoring of contractors for safety aspects. It was to anticipate problems and verify application of the decisions taken. Accordingly, an average of 30 checks was performed per month. The frequency of such checks depended on the extent of the work and the nature of the risks.

Each building had its own working group, which had the role of distributing the means of protection among the various trades and managing co-activity.

Another very important function of this unit was to examine safety and health protection plans. Each contractor had to submit its safety plan to the building coordinator. Some works were stopped until the plans and measures had been approved by the coordinators. A general inter-company safety and health plan was integrated into the general site coordination plan.

<u>Organisation of site health, safety and security infrastructure</u>

The other innovation lies in the fact that the client took charge of the general infrastructure of the site before the contractors arrived, and site management throughout the whole operation. The players were given the best possible conditions to contribute actively to implementation of the system.

- Everything needed for staff comfort and hygiene, such as the sanitary and utility blocks, for example, had been installed on the land before the start of

---

(⁶) Number of lost days per 1 000 working hours.
(⁷) At the end of the works this unit was disbanded, but some of the members were hired by Renault and the work condition engineer is now running the working condition department of the whole site.

the work. The living quarters, designed for 2 000 people, were managed by Renault who invoiced their cost to the contractors working on its site.

- A first aid post was installed on the site, with its occupational physician, nurses, an ambulance and a helicopter pad. The nurses had a secondary role of providing first aid training for the personnel on the site. The first aid post received all accident victims, keeping the legal registers and statistics of the number of accidents by contractor.

- Reception of the personnel and enterprises. This is an obligation for the company, but in this case it went further than required by the rules and did better. The reception was an opportunity to present the site, give a reminder of basic safety instructions and more specific site instructions, to identify the personnel and hand them a badge. A welcome booklet was handed out to the contractors and their employees.

- Construction of all access roads on the entire site before the start of site work, which represented a preliminary investment by the client but which had the advantage of enabling safe travel during execution of the site work. Similarly, the land was prepared before building the structures, making it possible and easier to use platforms for construction of the building itself. Great attention was paid to prevention of falls from heights.

- Presence on the site of an ANPE branch (employment centre), and several firms renting equipment (platforms) and tooling (which could supply only approved equipment).

Functioning: The contractors were selected by invitation to tender with two preliminary short-listing stages. The first stage involved analysing the accident frequency and severity rates and occupational injury contributions over the past five years. Then the short-listed firms performed a safety self-assessment based on a questionnaire with a maximum score of 3 000 points. This self-assessment questionnaire could be challenged. If a dispute happened, an independent body would have conducted an audit according to the NFX 50-136-1 and ISO 9004 rules. The dispute's loser being charged the fee. Those firms having the average were approved and could submit a tender. Those who obtained a lower score could catch up if they were awarded a contract, but by meeting additional obligations (e.g. hiring a safety engineer).

Control of subcontracting firms and objectives: The prevention unit carried out a monitoring action. This control also concerned the data submitted by the firms each week and each month, which were compared with the statistics prepared by the first aid post. After processing, these data were published, which confirms the transparency of the procedure. The monthly follow-up of accident frequency and severity rates was ensured, and if any drift relative to the initial objectives set at the beginning of the project was observed the contractors would be financially penalised.

Renault used the tool of economic incentives with the contractors, asking them to provide for three safety officers in their budget forecasts. The budgeted cost was broken down as a pro rata of the turnover generated on the site by the contractors involved. The objective was to assign two officers and go no further if the accident frequency stabilised below 15, allowing the contractors to do without the third safety officer.

5.2.4. Experiences

Originality: The strong involvement of the client, Renault, should be emphasised. Renault wanted to have control of the management of its site and took numerous initiatives along these lines. In each of the numerous agreements signed with the players, a reminder was given of the commitment to safety. The detailed organisation of the site translated into planning of the successive work stages according to safety criteria. This was illustrated by the construction of roads at start-up of the site and preparation of the land before erection of the buildings. Moreover, due to the length of work on site, experience was acquired and progress was made especially for the last two buildings.

Experience of supplier: The experience was viewed positively by the suppliers. Some regret the loss of this supervision afterwards. The personnel and contractors were first surprised by the discipline demanded, and some constraints were well accepted. On the whole, the fact of being recognised as competent professionals was appreciated. The quality of the work environment and the availability at the site of technical facilities such as lifting platform renters were compensation for the discipline demanded. A slide show was shown to each contractor and each staff member when they first arrived on the site. This presentation gave an overview of the site, but also had the advantage of providing incoming personnel with a reminder of the safety rules.

5.2.5. Impressions of the effectiveness and scale of application

Renault's objectives were attained and this system is a response to the problem posed by a temporary, heterogeneous grouping of contractors. There was no fatal accidents. The accident frequency, for which the objective set was 15, was in fact 28 for the site as a whole. However, this rate fell to 17 for the last building. The severity rate, set at 0.60, was in fact 0.80.

'The constant steadiness of Renault did help us to reach the initial objectives.'

Mr F. Villa — Cramif Occupational Safety Officer

The subcontracting enterprises then went their separate ways on completion of the site, and it is hard to assess the impact of these measures on the firms that worked on the site.

The players interviewed for this case study consider that the key factor for the success lies in the involvement of the client and the overall approach to site management. The presence of a permanent prevention unit on the spot is the second key factor in this success. The economic interest of the company remains very much present and explains the constant determination to go further. The role of the safety and health bodies in charge of safety at work is also essential and can take the form of a partnership with the client as of the project launching stage.

5.2.6. Further information

Mr Serge Desgranges, Renault, Conditions de vie au travail, Établissement de Guyancourt, Service 67035, Address: TCR AVA 1.74; 1 avenue du Golf, F-78288 Guyancourt. Tel. (33) 134 95 42 01; fax (33) 134 95 45 70

5.3 PROCUREMENT IN THE ELECTRICITY SECTOR — ELECTRABEL

- *Belgium*
- *Legislative requirements regarding procurement*
- *Besacc*
- *Administration and organisation*

5.3.1. Background

According to Belgian occupational health and safety legislation (the Belgium Act on well-being at work of 4 August 1996) client companies must not use contractors who fail to respect workplace health and safety rules. This requirement is valid in situations where several companies are working together at a single location or where one company (client) hires in another (contractor) to perform specific tasks.

To illustrate how companies organise themselves and set up requirements when purchasing products or hiring contractors, interviews have been carried out with the Belgian company Electrabel. The legislation however does not specify how a client company is supposed to go about excluding unsafe contractors. The options include checking the contractor's references, asking for documentation, (annual reports, etc.), carrying out its own evaluation or requiring certification. In Belgium there are two major systems of certification of contractors. In the first place, there is VCA. The 'Veiligheids Checklist Aannemers' (contractor safety list) is a certification system for contractors drawn up in the Dutch petrochemical industry. It has been widely adopted by contractors and their clients in Belgium. In order to extend the certification approach to more branches, the Confederation of Belgian Industry (Verbond van Belgische Ondernemingen — VBO/Fédération des Entreprises de Belgique — FEB) developed a platform for defining criteria for evaluation of contractors. Clients, contractors and government were involved in drafting the list. This was done in order to establish uniform criteria that could be applied to all sectors. The outcome was the 'Belgian safety criteria for contractors' (Besacc). The main differences between the two systems are shown in the following table.

The main differences between the two systems Besacc and VCA are:

Besacc	VCA
The Besacc system is meant for all activities including those with minor risks.	The system is specially aimed at subcontractors who deliver services or carry out so called 'high risk' activities or hazardous work.
Includes a checklist with safety criteria based on the European framework directive on health and safety at work (89/391/EEC). Furthermore a translation of the Act on well-being at work of the 4 August 1996 is included.	Includes a checklist with safety criteria based on the European framework directive on health and safety at work (89/391/EEC).
The evaluation is carried out by a group of safety experts with experience in safety matters. The requested documents have to prove that the criteria for safe subcontracting are fulfilled.	The evaluation of the VCA system includes the compiled documentation as well as the results of an audit executed by a certified institute.

Purchasing

Furthermore the principles for purchasing machines and collective and personal safety equipment are described in the Belgian regulations: code on well-being at work with the 'royal decrees on work equipment and personal protective equipment' on the one hand and, for collective protection, 'the older general regulations for work protection' on the other).

Electrabel is the main electricity producing and distribution company in Belgium. The head office of Electrabel is situated in Brussels. The other company locations of Electrabel are spread over the entire country. Because of the nature of its work, Electrabel can act as both client and contractor. Electrabel is a company who's new policy is to source out the maintenance activities and activities which aren't core business and thereby act as client. The maintenance activities in the three operations (generation, transport and distribution) are being increasingly outsourced, which will result in more frequent hiring of contractors. In the role of contractor they install and maintain the electricity grid for third parties. An objective of the Electrabel general safety plan is that within five years all Electrabel departments and subdepartments must have obtained a Besacc attestation or a VCA certificate.

The opening-up of the European energy market has had its strongest impact on the transport operations, which very likely will develop into an independent company in the future. The distribution operations are also developing into a structure where the network operations and the customer-related operations are becoming independent of one another. Another trend in line with this development is that the maintenance activities in the three operations (generation, transport and distribution) are being increasingly outsourced, which will result in more frequent hiring of contractors.

General organisational structure of Electrabel

Electrabel has three divisions according to the specific nature of the generation- and distribution-related activities: generation, transport and distribution.

The generation division consists of two nuclear generating stations, and traditionally fired generating stations, which are subdivided into seven operating zones and six maintenance zones. The transport division is structured according to three entities: north zone maintenance, south zone maintenance and support services (head office). Distribution is divided into three regions: a Flemish, Walloon and Central region. Each of the three distribution divisions is divided into zones (2–6 zones). The human resources and marketing divisions provide advice to all these divisions.

The structure of the company has an important influence on the organisation and operation of the Internal Service for Prevention and Protection at Work. The Internal Service for Prevention and Protection at Work consists of a central department that reports directly to the managing director and a local department in each zone. In the internal service there are several prevention advisers.

The central department of the Internal Service for Prevention and Protection at Work develops the general safety directives and strategies while the local departments implement them according to the specific nature of their operations. In order to streamline the safety policy, coordination meetings are held between the central department and the local departments.

5.3.2. Focus on occupational safety and health

Focus is to ensure compliance with the legislative directives and principles regarding procurement.

5.3.3. Current use of the system

Procurement of services

When the departments are requested, the contractors are inspected to see that they can perform their work safely.

'Having a Besacc attestation or a VCA certificate is an important criterion for selecting the contractor.'

M. J. De Ranter: Service de prévention Centrale

Having a Besacc attestation or a VCA certificate is an important criterion for selecting the contractor (although this is not yet compulsory). However Besacc and VCA are only one way of proving that the criteria for safe subcontracting are met. A company that can prove that its safety policy is at least as good as the discussed systems will not be excluded from working with Electrabel (e.g. OSHAS management system).

The contractor is first informed about the dangers inherent to Electrabel's operations. The implementation of the works is inspected and then the works themselves are evaluated.

This general procedure is supposed to be applied with every purchase or service provided, but this is not yet always possible in practice.

The company has switched to the SAP (systems, applications and products in data processing) system for the entire administrative management. SAP services support the IT infrastructure to help enterprises to meet their company objectives. The system integrates all data necessary to meet these objectives.

This system can be customised and has been partially rewritten to include safety procedures. The administrative management system is only accessible in a semi-centralised manner (still divided per division and their departments), but this has also led to greater uniformity of the safety system and procedures, and to better control of the implementation and monitoring of the purchasing procedures.

Procurement of products

The staff and the purchasing department has produced a list together with the Internal Service for Prevention and Protection at Work, which specifies:

1. which products may be freely purchased by the purchasing department;
2. which products may only be purchased after prior advice from the prevention adviser;
3. which products may only be purchased after a thorough examination by the staff.

The Internal Service for Prevention and Protection at Work uses the list to decide whether a product belongs to category 1, 2 or 3. The examination depends of the fact that the product is new, unknown, probably dangerous, etc.

New products are always subject to a risk evaluation and, depending on the result, additional requirements can be placed on them, which go further than the minimum safety requirements.

The prevailing legislation (e.g. Royal Decree on machines, Royal Decree on work equipment, etc.) and the requirements relevant for the purchasing department are also included in this system. Furthermore, files have been compiled for a large number of specific products (e.g. drilling machines) which set out all the safety requirements for the types to be purchased.

The practical organisation and administration

The purchasing department is organised into business units where the general safety strategy is determined centrally, but where the practical implementation can vary depending on the specific nature of the activity concerned.

The educational level of the co-workers from the purchasing department varies from secondary education to university education, with around 50 employees per business unit (there are six business units in total). The prevention advisers, the future users (in particular the staff) and the purchasing department are involved in drafting the safety requirements.

When negotiating a contract for purchases of products or services the main players, depending on the specific nature of the products or service, are:

- the local department of the Internal Service for Prevention and Protection at Work;
- the purchasing department;
- the staff.

'The inclusion of safety requirements into the purchasing procedures has meant that new risks are avoided in the best cases, and that they can always be better managed in the other case.'

M. M. Bollansée: Service de prévention de DOEL

When considering alternatives for products or services, the local department of the Internal Service for Prevention and Protection and the purchasing department are mainly involved. Examining whether the products or services satisfy the safety requirements is a matter for the local prevention advisers and the purchasing department.

In the consultations for a contract, the price, safety and quality are examined and given equal weight. Safety aspects that are taken into consideration are, for example:
- user friendliness and comfort;
- possible damage to health and the environment;
- safe working conditions for the suppliers or contractors.

Depending on the specific nature of the product to be purchased or the service to be provided, certificates will be requested from the suppliers: third-party certificates (e.g. inspection bodies), and all certificates and reports in accordance with the CE marking directive.

When a product comes in it is checked to see whether it satisfies the set specifications according to the requirements given on the order form, and whether the requested documents are attached. For specific products, it is requested that the prevention advisers drafts a service report before it comes into use; this is however not always possible in practice.

'If the supplied product does not satisfy the set specifications, the invoice will not be paid.'

Madame M. Coucke: Service d'achats de DOEL

If the supplied product does not satisfy the set specifications, the invoice will not be paid. The purchasing organisation and administration has become more visible and controllable through the introduction of the SAP system.

Information and training

The various players in the purchasing domain are informed about the safety procedures and requirements that apply to the company. To keep up with the legal requirements and to inform the managers about the changing legislation is hard to manage and control. There is a large flow of information that has to be supervised. The training given to managers and other employees aims mainly at clarifying the changes in the national legislation (the Royal Decrees on machines and personal protective equipment, the Act on well-being at work and related royal decrees such as the Royal Decree on well-being policy or the Royal Decree on work equipment) and related practical requirements.

External companies that supply products or services to Electrabel are informed about the risks and working processes within Electrabel, the safety procedures used, etc. For each business unit there is an evaluation system for barring or excluding contractors or suppliers. The exclusion criteria are built up step by step, with the last stage being exclusion.

Contractors are first asked whether they have a VCA certificate or a Besacc attestation (these are not yet compulsory) or are using any other safety management system.

Training is currently given to the staff and to contractors.

5.3.4. Experiences

The users of the products and services are generally positive towards the safety requirements. Safety control on products and services gives a greater confidence in the quality of these goods. While the suppliers have responded neither positively nor negatively, contractors view the safety requirements in a rather positive light, in the way that those who satisfy the criteria for safe subcontracting have an advantage compared to those who don't. The exclusion of unreliable suppliers or contractors plays in the favour of those who can satisfy the requirements. The exclusion percentage is estimated to be around 3 %.

The exclusion of certain suppliers or contractors has led to minor internal conflicts in some cases.

5.3.5. Impression of effectiveness and scale of application

The safety measures result in fewer violations of the law. The system guarantees safer incoming products and services. The inclusion of safety requirements in the purchasing procedures has led to better risk management.

The system satisfies the set objective: better risk management. It can also be said that the safety level of products and services has increased.

The safety system, which has a legal foundation, applies to the various operations of the company and seems applicable also for other companies.

Companies in Belgium have been asked/required to aim for better risk management for many years now, and to bar risks at the company gate in a manner of speaking. Over the years this has lead to better quality without prices being substantially influenced by it.

5.3.6. Further information

Mr Jan De Ranter, Electrabel, Regentlaan 8, B-1000 Brussels. Tel. (32-2) 518 67 62; fax (32-2) 213 52 44; e-mail: jan.deranter@electrabel.com

5.4 PROCUREMENT IN THE PHARMACEUTICAL INDUSTRY — ASTRAZENECA MANAGEMENT CONCEPT

- United Kingdom
- SHE policy
- SHE management standards
- Purchasing requirements
- Audit of contractors
- Vendor rating system
- Total cost ownership

5.4.1. Background

AstraZeneca is one of the world's leading pharmaceutical companies. The company was formed in April 1999 by the merger of Astra AB of Sweden and Zeneca Group PLC of the UK, both companies with strong traditions in safety, health and environment (SHE) work. Zeneca was demerged from ICI, a large chemical company involved in a whole range of commodity and speciality products and therefore had a history of attention to safety and health issues. Astra on the other hand was very much focused on environmental issues. AstraZeneca's mission is to be first for innovation and value in the provision of products and services to improve health and quality of life. Safety, health and environmental considerations are core to this and all AstraZeneca's activities must be in accordance with the SHE policy and shall take into account the SHE management standards. The SHE policy and the eight SHE management standards apply to the whole company and were agreed upon before the actual merger was a reality so that they would be in place from day one of the new company.

AstraZeneca's eight management standards:

1. responsibilities and commitment;
2. management of SHE;
3. communications and consultations;
4. risk management;
5. environmental impact reduction;
6. contractors, toll manufacturers and suppliers;
7. SHE auditing and monitoring;
8. annual review and improvement plans.

eight new SHE standards, which were developed over a period of five months, leave room for implementation of local procedures reflecting local conditions and specific needs.

It is acknowledged throughout the company that SHE management is only effective when managers show that they have a personal interest in maintaining and improving performance. This is also reflected in the job description for the senior executive team. Part of their job description relates to their SHE responsibilities. Senior managers throughout the group are accountable for ensuring that the activities under their control are carried out in accordance with the AstraZeneca SHE policy. They shall ensure that an appropriate organisation, with defined responsibilities and accountabilities is established, and that the skills and resources necessary to implement the policy are in place.

A number of activities based on the SHE policy and the SHE management standards have been systematised by the company and are compatible with the principles in ISO 14001, the environmental management system, and are illustrated in an AstraZeneca leaflet explaining the whole performance cycle as shown below.

Principles are based on continuous improvements and local implementation at each site. All sites and locations are required to have a management system in place, which is communicated to all staff and external contractors working at the sites.

'I firmly believe that a good safety, health and environmental performance is not something that is "nice to have" nor is it just the responsibility of our professional SHE staff. It is an integral part of everything we do and it is the personal responsibility of each of us to make sure that we do it well.'

Tom McKillop, Chief Executive in his July 1999 announcement of the annual SHE awards

1. **How committed are we?** Policy, standards, guidelines
2. **What are we doing?** Corporate objectives & targets
3. **What's your role?** Local implementation
4. **How do we check?** Auditing
5. **What have we achieved?** Reporting
6. **Is it satisfactory?** Management review
7. **Who needs to know?** Communication

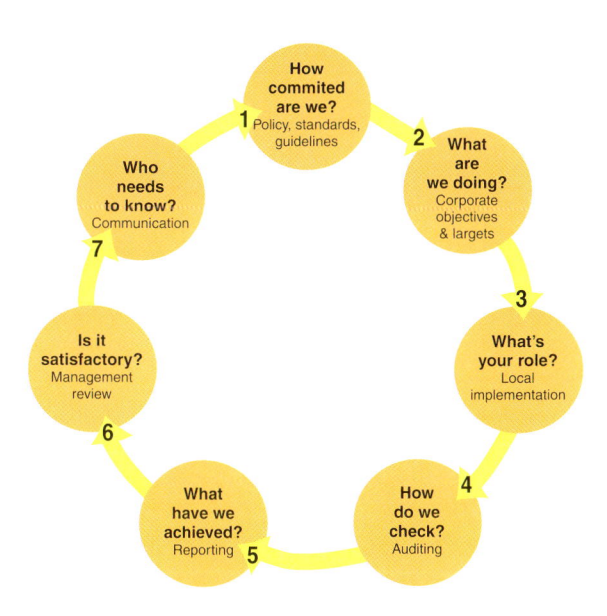

Compared to the 19 SHE standards implemented by the old Zeneca Group PLC, AstraZeneca has introduced fewer and less detailed standards. Zeneca learned from experience that too many standards could be confusing, as all of them were not relevant for every site and thereby made it difficult to comply. The

AstraZeneca is in partnership with a large number of other people and organisations who supply it with products and services. AstraZeneca purchases all kinds of equipment and services. Services include, among others, grass cutting, training of people and building chemical plants. Sometimes services are performed at AstraZeneca and sometimes outside the premises. Vendors which fulfil the requirements from AstraZeneca are entered on a list of preferred vendors.

One of AstraZeneca's eight standards deals with contractors, toll manufacturers and suppliers and is, like all standards, supplemented with guidelines and commentaries for the managers expanding on the contents and including questions for managers to consider.

> **SHE Standard No. 6: Contractors, toll manufacturers and suppliers**
> SHE considerations shall be taken into account during the selection of contractors, toll manufacturers and suppliers to ensure that competent partners are selected.
> There shall be an exchange of SHE information and requirements between AstraZeneca and any partner to ensure that the requirements for safe conditions and protection of the environment are met. Subsequently, performance shall be monitored to ensure that AstraZeneca's requirements are fulfilled.

As the performance of these organisations may directly affect AstraZeneca's operations and reputation, the company finds it is necessary that there is a clear understanding between local managers and the contractors as to how the responsibilities for managing SHE issues is shared and performance is monitored.

SHE considerations are therefore an integrated element in all purchasing situations. This is supported by the organisational structure of the company where the corporate SHE support is led by the Vice President for SHE, Engineering and Purchasing. The corporate SHE department is a discrete department which is not directly involved in the purchasing situations but is setting the standards to be met by potential suppliers, toll manufacturers and contractors. The various functions then have to demonstrate what actions they will take to meet these standards. The SHE department will support with consultancy and advice if needed.

AstraZeneca has established a purchasing network in the UK, which is led by the Head of Commercial Services Department. Equivalent networks are operating in Sweden and the US, and they are all part of a global network with a UK-based leadership group.

5.4.2. Focus on occupational safety and health

Healthy business depends on a healthy staff and a continuous supply and stable performance of suppliers, toll manufacturers and contract workers. This is why AstraZeneca makes great efforts to select and monitor their business partners among those who can demonstrate a high level of SHE performance.

AstraZeneca has introduced a total cost ownership (TCO) principle, which is applied in purchasing situations. TCO means that products are looked at in a life-cycle perspective and that also SHE aspects are considered in relation to all phases of the product cycle in the company and not only the use phase.

All purchasing is therefore done in multifunctional teams and their contribution will be part of the record for the purchasing activity.

Senior representatives from purchasing, engineering, SHE, manufacturing, supply chain management and human resources have meetings every two weeks, where evaluations of purchasing activities and SHE-related issues in general are discussed.

Purchasing requirements when buying goods

When AstraZeneca is buying goods the OSH requirements are written into the specifications of the goods. For example, specifications for machines and office equipment will include ergonomic aspects as well as more usual operating requirements. Machines and other larger pieces of equipment have to pass a factory acceptance test, which also involves SHE parameters. A user representative will be involved in the planning and implementation of the test. Suppliers of goods are not monitored with regard to their safety and health performance in their own company.

Purchasing requirements when buying services

When buying services potential suppliers are prequalified and will not be employed if they cannot demonstrate good safety and health performance. If they do not have the right SHE approach this is expected to affect their performance and reliability as a supplier.

'AstraZeneca would never sacrifice safety and health for the sake of a commercial decision in a purchasing situation.'

Geoff Aldcroft, Head of Commercial Services Department Statement during interview in May 2000

Safety and health auditing of potential suppliers

Safety:
- safe systems of work;
- induction/refresher training;
- personal protective equipment;
- fire detection and protection systems;
- chemical and operational hazard procedures;
- guarding of equipment, e.g. drive shafts, pulleys, etc.;
- materials of construction, maintenance policy;
- accident statistics, investigations, improvement plans.

Health:
- medical checks/history;
- workplace environmental monitoring for noise, dust, solvents and gases;
- working hours including shift patterns;
- health/welfare programmes, either available on site or in locality

Both contractors working at AstraZeneca's premises and outside the premises are audited with regard to their SHE performance, although more attention is put on the contractors working at the premises. An example from a checklist of safety and health issues covered by such an audit is shown in the box.

Audits are performed as part of the prequalification procedure for contractors and also regularly every year during the actual contract work. Potential suppliers get verbal feedback at the end of the audit. Observations are also put down in writing and areas that need improvement are noted in the written feedback. During the actual contract work there are regular meetings with the contractors and Contractor Safety and Health Committee meetings are arranged every month. New contractors go through an induction programme presenting the AstraZeneca requirements for safety and health at work. This induction programme lasts two hours for contractors working a shorter period at the premises. A full day course is offered for contract workers with an assignment lasting one week or more. This also forces the contractors to use the same workforce for assignments at AstraZeneca. All contract workers receive refresher training when they are involved over a longer period. Induction and refresher courses are conducted by the local SHE groups. Term contractors who provide services over several years have to provide safety and health plans and plans for improvement to the site manager.

AstraZeneca has introduced a vendor rating system. The rating system expresses the basic confidence in the supplier. It does not include specific safety and health elements but safety and health can be a differentiator. Potential suppliers are divided into three categories. First category suppliers fulfil the requirements. Suppliers in the second category are encouraged to move up into the first category. Third category suppliers are not fulfilling the requirements and are excluded.

In addition AstraZeneca has introduced a whole series of activities to encourage good safety and health work and keep things moving and improving. Safety competitions and SHE awards based on accident reporting and audit results are such examples.

5.4.3. Current use of scheme

The SHE management system, consisting of the SHE policy, the management standards and the related guidelines, was developed by AstraZeneca building on the many years of experience with successful management of occupational safety and health in the two merged companies. The monitoring system for suppliers, toll manufacturers and contract workers and especially the audit scheme, which is part of the system, is to the knowledge of the corporate SHE group not used in any other pharmaceutical companies.

The AstraZeneca SHE performance cycle shares the same basic principles of continuous improvements with the ISO 14001 standard.

5.4.4. Experiences

The AstraZeneca policy on international standards like ISO 14001 is not to promote it across the company, but any individual site can seek certification.

External evaluation of AstraZeneca's management system by external auditors has shown that it more than meets the criteria for ISO certification.

Corporate Health and Safety Group's experience

According to the Corporate Safety and Health Group the whole approach to and focus on SHE issues, and the commitment from senior management in the company, supports an effective SHE culture. Suppliers, toll manufacturers and contract workers are met with a number of requirements in the purchasing situation and through supervision and auditing of their safety and health performance during work. The strong focus on their SHE performance also influences the focus on safety and health among the internal staff.

Low accident rates among company staff and contractors at the premises are considered a direct result of this work. The AstraZeneca board has set a target of zero accidents and zero incidents, realising that this is an aspirational target and may be difficult to achieve. However, AstraZeneca believes that accepting a certain rate of accidents and incidents does not lead to the behavioural changes that are needed to achieve real improvement.

The Corporate Safety and Health Group also acknowledges that AstraZeneca is still a new organisation, and not all procedures are fully implemented and in place in the merged company. The new organisation is still striving to integrate the two slightly different SHE cultures from Astra and Zeneca, but they find that it has been a major advantage that the SHE management system was in place before the actual merger.

Purchasers' experience

Three people involved in purchasing, including the head of commercial services department, have been interviewed. They all expressed that AstraZeneca will not compromise safety in a purchasing situation. If there is a cheaper alternative from a supplier with lower SHE standards compared to AstraZeneca's, they will work with the supplier to see what could be improved and try to encourage them to do so. This is also to ensure future supply. Knowing the total cost implications in relation to occupational injuries, AstraZeneca never buys from companies who do not fulfil legislative requirements. Apparently cheaper items are not always cheaper when looking at the true costs as it is the case when applying the total cost ownership principle.

There are however situations where certain chemicals are prescribed which are only available from companies with a lower rating. In these situations AstraZeneca will also try to encourage the supplier to improve. In general they will pay more attention to the services with regard to contractors own working environment.

The purchasing representatives interviewed mentioned a few areas where they found that improvements were needed. As every site manager is responsible for implementation of the SHE management system locally, vendors may meet different standards for SHE work in different departments. This is not desirable, as contract workers must expect to operate to one standard. AstraZeneca is working on improving this situation and an outsourcing/procurement group has been established with the purpose of giving a more consistent message to the suppliers. One of the ways to meet this requirement is to have one person assigned to audit a specific supplier instead of the individual departments.

It was mentioned that there were no formal discussions or meetings between the auditors and the SHE group and that safety audit reports were not available centrally, e.g. in a database. This was suggested as an area for improvement.

The head of the UK's commercial services department was of the general opinion that the SHE culture and activities in the company did result in a happier workforce as well as fewer accidents and work-related illnesses among contractors and the company's own staff.

Suppliers' experience

No suppliers have been interviewed, but generally AstraZeneca experiences a positive reaction from the suppliers to the company's requirements. Many suppliers make quite an effort to be entered on the list of preferred vendors. Suppliers also benefit from the consultation and feedback they get as part of the auditing system for potential suppliers.

5.4.5. Impression of the effectiveness and scale of application

Interviewing people in different positions within AstraZeneca leaves the impression that occupational safety and health has a very high priority and is based on a strong commitment from senior management. Integration of SHE considerations in the purchasing situation, conducting audits and monitoring contractors seems to improve the SHE performance not only among the contractors but also among AstraZeneca's own staff. This is largely due to the visible demonstration of the importance of complying with the SHE management system in daily work.

The system seems to work in a dynamic and informal way, which contributes to the identified positive results, e.g. in the form of improved accident rates.

As the management system is implemented locally, site managers play an important role, also because coordination between the different sites and exchange of audit experience is less formalised. This could be an area for improvement.

In principle the AstraZeneca SHE management concepts are applicable to all types of industries that are dependent on stable suppliers, toll manufacturers and contract workers. Especially the pharmaceutical industry which is commercially and environmentally sensible and has a strong need for a systematic and reliable approach to safety, health and environment. They must therefore be expected to have the necessary support and backup from senior management which is crucial to the success of any management system.

5.4.6. Further information

Further information regarding the SHE management system at AstraZeneca can be obtained from the Corporate Director for Health and Safety, Chief Medical Director, Eric Teasdale, AstraZeneca, Alderley House, Alderley Park, Macclesfield, Cheshire SK10 4TF, England. Tel. (44-1625) 58 28 28

6.

OSH IN GENERIC PROCUREMENT SYSTEMS

6.1 PROCUREMENT OF CLEANING AGENTS — IKA

- Denmark
- Procurement of universal cleaning agents
- OSH focus in tender material
- Assistance to purchasers
- Public procurement

6.1.1. Background

This case study describes an example of guidelines used to define requirements in tenders for procurement of cleaning agents.

The guidelines are produced by a working group appointed by The Association of Public Purchasers in Denmark (IKA). This working group consists of three people representing public purchasers, and three suppliers and one person representing the Association of Danish Manufactures and Importers of Soap, Detergents, Perfume, Cosmetics and Chemical Technical Products (SPT).

As part of the development process, the guidelines have been discussed with representatives from the Danish Working Environment Authority.

The purpose of the guidelines is to:

- assist purchasers in order to ensure that all relevant requirements regarding the delivery of cleaning agents are included when tenders are prepared;
- stimulate suppliers to develop more environmentally and occupationally safe cleaning agents;
- save time for purchasers when preparing tenders by offering a fill-in template for the tender;
- save time for purchasers when evaluating tenders based on standardised questions asked to the tenderers;
- save time for the suppliers of cleaning agents as a result of standardised requirements from more purchasers.

6.1.2. Focus on occupational safety and health

The guidelines include requirements relevant for both the safety and health of the cleaning staff and for the external environment. The requirements have been ranked with regard to price, function, environmental impact and occupational safety and health aspects. According to the requirements relevant to occupational safety and health, the cleaning agents may not:

- be marketed in the form of powder or aerosol spray;
- contain dangerous substances in keeping with Danish labelling criteria;
- contain specific detergents and complex binders;
- contain substances listed as carcinogenic, harmful for reproduction, allergenic or neurotoxic by the Danish Working Environment Authority;
- in general contain perfume, colours and product stabilisers.

The tenderers are asked to deliver information on all substances contained in the cleaning agents to the Danish Occupational Health Service (OHS) Centre in order to see if the cleaning agents fulfil the requirements.

With the purpose of testing the cleaning products, the suppliers are sometimes asked to deliver samples of the products in question.

6.1.3. Current use of the scheme

The guidelines were developed in 1996 and at present they are only used in Denmark. The guidelines are available in Danish and are protected by copyright. IKA is considering translating the guidelines into English. Up to February 2000 they have been revised three times. The guidelines are primarily used by purchasers in public institutions when purchasing cleaning agents for cleaning of public offices and institutions like schools, hospitals, etc. The developers estimate that the guidelines have been used for approximately 75 tenders prepared by municipalities and 12 tenders prepared by counties up to February 2000. The guidelines and the requirements are also available on a floppy disc. Text is in Word, Windows version 2.0 and calculations in Excel. The material is designed as a fill-in template and the tenderers can formulate their tenders directly in the fill-in template. In total the material comprises 22 A4 pages, including appendices. The experiences using the scheme are elaborated in the following.

6.1.4. Experiences

The IKA working group evaluates that use of the guidelines has resulted in:

- a product development leading to more occupationally and environmentally safe cleaning agents;
- less decentralised procurement in the public institutions and therefore more certainty that cleaning agents fulfil the outlined requirements;
- less time consuming processes in relation to preparation of tenders and evaluation of tenders.

The purchasers stress that they have saved time using the guidelines' requirements. Especially when they prepare tender materials.

A representative from an Occupational Health Service Centre, who has evaluated whether the cleaning agents fulfil the requirements, believes that the guidelines have:

- forced suppliers to consider whether their cleaning agents fulfil the requirements and hereby strengthened focus on impact of the cleaning agents and on the occupational safety and health;
- resulted in increasing use of cleaning agents deriving from 'green' product lines;
- motivated the suppliers to deliver information about recipes;
- standardised the form in which the information is delivered by the suppliers and hereby made the OHS Centre assessment more efficient.

Purchasers' experience

Based on response from cleaners, it seems that they mainly react positively to the fact that cleaning agents should fulfil the above-mentioned requirements. For the manager of the cleaning staff it is important that the cleaning agents are purchased with the focus on the safety and health of the cleaning staff. The manager expresses that this allows for greater confidence in the job. The cleaner is also positive to the scheme, though it is difficult to say if the working environment has been improved because of the requirements set up in the purchasing situation. It is therefore difficult for the individual cleaner to see a direct relation between the 'new' cleaning agents and a better working environment. If, for example, a cleaner does not suffer from allergy or is easily sensitised, the fact that the 'new' cleaning agents do not contain allergens will not automatically be recognised as an improvement. Only on a longer term, statistics may show that fewer cleaners become allergic to cleaning agents.

'Cleaning staff should always be asked to test the cleaning agents before any purchase commitments are taken, since the cleaning staff are the ones using the products.'

Pia Mathiasen, Cleaner with the Danish Municipality Ishøj. Questionnaire response, March 2000

A few purchasers have also been asked about their experiences using the guidelines. Their responses indicate that they are satisfied with the guidelines and they stress that using the guidelines' requirements has been less time consuming. Especially when the tender material is prepared, because the guidelines include relevant requirements to be forwarded to the invited tenders. However, one of the purchasers stated that the guidelines are not sufficient when proposals should be compared. He finds that an expert in cleaning agents should be consulted and that assistance is necessary if the different proposals fulfil different parts of the requirements and a priority ranking is necessary. This, in spite of the fact that the proposals are more uniform and a comparison of the proposals is less time consuming after using the guidelines. Purchasers find it important to emphasise the health and environmental product development and that more purchasers using similar requirements will stimulate this process. The purchasers have had no responses from cleaners indicating that the 'new' cleaning agents are less effective than the old ones. However, one purchaser was confronted with the criticism that products without perfume for cleaning toilets are not very pleasant to use.

Suppliers' experience

When the guidelines were developed, the suppliers were represented through their trade organisation SPT. SPT was a little reluctant in the beginning because they knew the criteria might be difficult to fulfil for some of their member companies. However, by postponing the guidelines and hereby giving more time to product development, SPT has today a very positive approach to the guidelines. At present, SPT includes information about the guidelines and their requirements in training courses for suppliers.

In order to obtain more information, a manager representing a supplier has been asked about the company's attitude to the guidelines. The manager of product development replies that the company has lost contracts because their previous product assortment could not fulfil the OSH requirements of the purchasers. However, product development has been ongoing and today the manager of product development estimates that the company has gained market shares because they have been able to fulfil the OSH requirements. The manager stresses that by presenting realistic requirements, the guidelines have had a great influence on product development. In addition, the OSH requirements have forced the supplier to set up OSH requirements to their subsuppliers. The manager answers that both the company itself and the subsuppliers in general have reacted positively to the fact that customers meet them with OSH requirements.

> 'It has major influence on our development that the customers set up requirements. It is important too, that the requirements are realistic, because we attach great importance on the effectiveness of the products.'
>
> Annette Hansen, Head of Product Development Department, Multidrik in Denmark. Questionnaire response, April 2000

6.1.5. Impression of effectiveness and scale of application

The guidelines seem to have contributed to put more focus on the impact of cleaning agents on the occupational safety and health of the cleaning staff. The guidelines assist the tenderer to include appropriate requirements regarding the cleaning agents' environmental and occupational safety and health aspects. In a long-term perspective, the standardised requirements will encourage the suppliers to develop more cleaning agents fulfilling the requirements.

The guidelines are considered to be particularly applicable for:
- large companies preparing tenders for procurement of all kind of cleaning agents and public institutions, i.e. offices, schools, hospitals, etc.

6.1.6. Further information

More information: 'The guideline for tenders — requirements for cleaning agents' can be obtained from The IKA Secretariat, c/o Holstebro Kommune, DK-7500 Holstebro. Tel. (45) 96 11 70 43; fax (45) 96 11 70 52; e-mail: ika@holstebro.dk; Internet: www.ika.holstebro.dk

6.2 STIMULATING OSH PROCUREMENT — BESCHAFFUNGSSERVICE AUSTRIA

- Austria
- Public procurement
- OSH in purchasing guidelines
- Assistance to purchasers
- Networking among purchasers

Beschaffungs Service Austria

6.2.1. Background

In Austria there is strong emphasis on federal structures as well as the independence and responsibility of every public buyer — big or small. Thus there is no common purchasing policy in the public sector. The sector is made up by public entities on several levels:

- federal government;
- nine provincial governments;
- local (city/town/ village governments);
- independent institutions governed by public law (public health insurance bodies, companies owned by public entities, organisations formed by several independent entities for a particular purpose).

The total amount spent by public purchasers in Austria on all levels of government and public institutions in 1998 made up for 17 % of GDP. Due to procedural limitations purchasers are supposed to look for the most economic alternative available. By tradition, that usually meant the cheapest product or service available. Methodological problems contributed to the use of the price as the only indicator for economical quality, as the life-cycle approach still had to be developed. Formal regulations govern the tendering and purchasing processes. Any intervention to modify that, particularly where quality aspects are introduced, must ensure that formal and quality aspects are considered.

For more than 10 years IFZ (Interuniversitäres Forschungszentrum für Technik, Arbeit und Kultur) in Graz, a private institute operating in close connection with the Austrian universities joint IFF (Institut für Interdisziplinäre Forschung und Fortbildung), has made practical solutions for environmental issues as one of their key issues. Growing awareness in the public sector that the uncontrolled growth of waste posed long-term dangers demanded tools for a more professional approach. In 1997, the then Ministry for Families and the Environment looked for a partner institution to bundle and further develop existing knowledge in this field, and to integrate the cleaner production approach (among Austrian industry known under the trademark Ökoprofit). This resulted in the establishment of BeschaffungsService Austria within IFZ, with contributions from the ministry. The main task of BeschaffungsService Austria is to provide advise: BeschaffungsService Austria offers resources for purchasers, in the form of guidelines and information. In addition it is a centre for research and coordination of research. Furthermore BeschaffungsService acts as an interest institution, and meanwhile it provides a trademark for ecological purchasing in the public sector.

BeschaffungsService: Providing resources, networking, lobbying, trademarks

One of the basics of cleaner production is that organisations should become aware that an adequate purchasing policy is the first step towards prevention. Experts in the area of OSH often are confronted with the task of assessing problems produced by machinery, materials, structures and processes that were already purchased and/or laid out in the respective company. OSH experts apparently have difficulties in making themselves heard and giving advice during planning and decision-making stages. According to a safety expert and technology researcher with Austria's public ARCS institute, integrating SHE aspects into an organisation's management system, which is asked for by professionals in charge of ecological procurement, provided the opportunity to set up alliances for the benefit of the companies and their workers and environment.

Participating in development of procurement guidelines makes sense: 'A problem you don't buy you won't have'.

Toni Geyer, Technology Researcher and Safety Expert, ARCS, interview, August 2000

BeschaffungsService Austria and their ministerial counterparts soon realised that it was important to convince professionals that good purchasing also means environmentally sound (and eventually healthy) purchasing. By doing so the public procurement field could be changed on a broad scale.

The services provided by BeschaffungsService have been without charges or fees. BeschaffungsService's activities are supported by governmental grants.

6.2.2. Focus on occupational safety and health

Within the BeschaffungsService and with their counterparts' projects the main focus is on ecological purchasing. Issues related to health and safety are nevertheless gaining ground. Main areas where so called 'green' and health issues have been linked are the purchasing of:

- cleaning agents;
- paints;
- chemicals used in maintenance of machinery and vehicles;
- office furniture.

The weight to be attributed to OSH items within the BeschaffungsService framework is perceived differently by different actors. The ministry emphasises that OSH must be seen as an important and integral part of an elaborated procurement system. BeschaffungsService Austria finds that the integration of OSH into their approach is so far not substantial. However, some persons in charge of procurement at city level claim that OSH elements are already being considered more regularly. The newest example of a guideline is a criteria catalogue listing all items used for the interior of public buildings (ranging from floor materials to furniture) (Amerstorfer et al., Vienna 1999).

So far there has been little consideration for occupational safety and health issues beyond the buyer's system. In the city of Vienna however there is a clear intention to take a closer look at working conditions on the side of suppliers of services. This will mean development of guidelines for clarifying OSH issues in contracts, as well as for auditing and inspection. Both the city's and their suppliers' systems are obviously overlapping, for instance where cleaning of buildings is carried out by contractors, as a procurement official in Vienna points out. Adverse health effects caused by chemical agents (solvents, disinfectants) are of relevance for both the cleaning staff of the contractor company and the city employees.

Awareness of health hazards thus can very well support the buyer's occupational safety and health organisation. An occupational physician remarks, that in general a state-of-the-art OSH system should look for health hazards and eliminate them in advance, before manifest health problems occur. The opportunity to join forces with environmentally sound buying procedures makes it easier to do so. This preventive approach becomes even more important, as the majority occupational health problems are long-term effects of unhealthy working conditions that nevertheless are quite common. Therefore it is important to act before ill health can be diagnosed in workers. As in the case of work-related allergies among cleaning personnel, it would be too late to intervene once the allergy appears. This focus on long-term hazards can be related to the life-cycle approach in assessing products environmentally.

Like a purchaser looking beyond a product's price, an occupational health professional must present an overall view when assessing health hazards. The OSH expert's activities therefore must include intervention into procurement processes, as companies and organisations must learn to avoid potential 'troublemakers' from the beginning. Troublemakers very often are not substances regulated by threshold limit values, nor technical appliances that are totally outlawed. Also chemical substances often are present in amounts below limit values and may damage a worker's health over the years. A VDU (visual display unit), correctly used with other furniture elements may in the long run lead to musculo-skeletal disorders, although there is no visible problem in the short term.

Also regarding paints and varnish used on furniture or floors, avoiding solvents is a common goal for OSH and environmentally oriented buyers. Although the amount of solvents released may be well below TLVs (threshold limit values), working in such an environment may cause harm and should be avoided. The use of substances with allergenic potential, for instance in cleaning agents, is not illegal, but may still lead to the development of skin allergies in cleaning staff. Thus occupational doctors look at the substances, and cooperation is useful to avoid bringing them into an organisation's system at all.

6.2.3. Current use of scheme

A series of guidelines for certain areas have been prepared, or are under preparation, covering areas as different as environmentally sound printing products,

products used in construction such as windows and pipes and energy saving lamps. Guidelines older than two years are being revised. BeschaffungsService is carrying out work on new guidelines either within their IFZ parent institute or in cooperation with experts from universities, private research institutes and experts of the provinces' environmental departments. In some cases suppliers' representatives (Chamber of Commerce) are included in the experts panels.

Studies and guidelines prepared by other members of the network have been published or distributed through BeschaffungsService. Marketing efforts for materials are carried out under the common headline 'Check it!'. Six modules will soon be available in paper and Internet versions:

- materials for offices and schools;
- electrical appliances;
- building construction;
- interior;
- water;
- washing and cleaning agents.

Most of those documents, as they were intended to support ecological purchasing, only contain general remarks relating to occupational safety and health. Reference is made to existing TLVs for certain chemicals (like formaldehyde in chipboard), in another case a guideline for ecological construction recommends avoiding solvents and heavy metals.

According to an assessment by BeschaffungsService Austria and Ministry of Agriculture representatives, based on responses from officials in procurement departments of public entities, there is growing acceptance of ecological buying in Austria's big cities. The capital Vienna has decided at the political level that ecological buying shall become standard for the whole of the city's yearly ATS 56 billion (more than EUR 4 billion) purchase budget (including construction). In cooperation with BeschaffungsService, in Vorarlberg province a regional network of purchasers is already functioning, trying successfully to spread out to smaller communities under the local trademark 'Ökoleitfaden Vorarlberg'. To support public buyers in the region, their material even incorporates provincial regulations on public procurement.

BeschaffungsService for the purpose of disseminating information publishes a newsletter 'Take it!' that is reporting developments in their network and bringing to attention new tools developed by a network member. 'Take it!' has been published four times a year since 1997, and is sent out free to public buyers, decision-makers, suppliers, and other interested parties.

6.2.4. Experiences

Purchasers' experience

Both the BeschaffungsService Austria and the Ministry of Agriculture's environmental department came to the following conclusions.

'Environmentally sound purchasing must become a professional standard for public buyers.'

Edith Kainz, Graz city administration procurement department, interview, August 2000

- The tendering and purchase processes are becoming more professional. Ecological and healthy purchasing policies by public bodies are becoming part of the professional practice and state-of-the-art. This development makes it possible for purchasers and decision-makers that are not involved personally in health and ecological issues to adopt changes in purchase policies on a sound basis.
- The positive impact of guidelines and other tools that are easy to apply by actors in public purchasing where a growing trend towards decentralisation otherwise might threaten standards that were already established.
- A shift from control to self-control on the suppliers' side, as suppliers are asked to offer goods in compliance with requirements and to certify that they do so.
- Big purchasers (city administrations of Vienna and Linz) have begun to announce major changes in policy (i.e. the ban on PVC products). Such moves provide incentives to producers and suppliers to develop products and services in line with those requirements. Subsequently a market emerges for ecologically and health-wise better products. This opens a road for smaller public and private buyers to ask for ecologically sound products.

Public discussion and increased awareness, such as towards solvents, encourage purchasers to modify their requirements. At the same time, the more foresighted suppliers and industrial or organisational users are encouraged to prepare themselves for an orderly change to new technologies. A chemical engineer and project manager in charge of the Austrian legs of two current projects financed by EU funds aim to replace solvents in cleaning processes in offset printing and metal industries, have encountered growing awareness both from suppliers of cleaning products, and from innovative organisations and companies.

The Vienna administration soon realised that a comprehensive approach was needed to develop ecological public purchasing. In order to combine resources of various departments concerned they decided to launch an organisational development project. A project organisation was set up to involve those departments that were directly concerned with changes in procurement policy and practice.

'Announcing clear priorities in procurement with regard to certain quality aspects helps alert suppliers to develop/ modify products and services in time.'

Georg Patak, Vienna city administration, procurement and waste management department, interview, August 2000

In order to develop guidelines for the whole city and make sure that participation and identification by officials gets high, Vienna undertook changing of the city's procurement priorities by ways of an organisational change project.

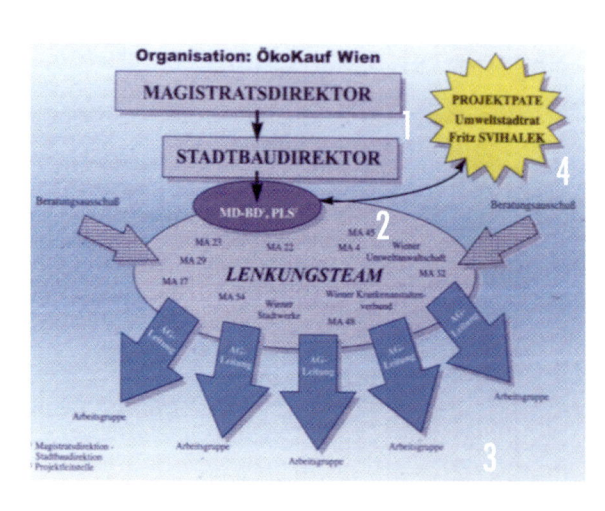

Organisation: ÖkoKauf Wien

1. Director / City administration; 2. Director / Construction department; 3. Project team; 4. Councillor for the Environment; 'MA' = department of the administration + department number.

Basic organisational structures have been revised. The project resulted in the formation of a network among various departments of the city administration. That network is in charge of planning and carrying out information and training activities, and enables the city's employees to work with these new guidelines. To make sure that the project can work under stable conditions, the council member in charge of the environmental policy in the city of Vienna was directly involved in the project.

6.2.5. Impression of the effectiveness and scale of application

Environmentally sound purchasing needs the development of user friendly guidelines, and checklists, based on sound knowledge. Existing knowledge needs to be increased, particularly regarding the life cycle of products as well as by health information.

Particular attention had to be paid to ensure that the tools developed were legally sound and products and services in public tenders were described correctly. This is of importance as purchasers must avoid allegations that they act against national and EU regulations governing markets and the behaviour of public institutions in those markets.

In addition, a common trademark that links similar approaches taking place in various independent entities is of great help, showing the stakeholders in such a process that there is a wider acceptance of that approach beyond the limits of their own organisation.

From an occupational physician's view, positive health effects can be expected in the long run.

The participation of OSH expertise within ecological procurement projects can strengthen the approach, adding a new quality.

'Occupational health and safety experts will be able to contribute a lot if they cooperate in developing procurement systems.'

Dr Brigitte Schigutt, occupational physician, AMD Centre for occupational medicine, Linz, interview, August 2000

6.2.6. Further information

Further information about BeschaffungsService Austria can be obtained from Dr Ines Öhme, IFZ Graz, Schlögelgasse 2, A-8010 Graz. Tel. (43-316) 813 90 99; fax (43 316) 81 02 74; e-mail: beschaffung@ifz.tu-graz.ac.at

6.3 STIMULATING OSH PROCUREMENT — VCA CHECKLIST

- *The Netherlands*
- *Contractor safety*
- *Certification of SHE management systems*
- *Certification of both small and large companies*

SHE
CHECKLIST
CONTRACTORS

6.3.1. Background

The Dutch VCA system (Veiligsheids Checklijst Aannemers) or in English the SCC scheme (SHE ([8]) checklist contractors) was developed in 1994 to objectively evaluate and certify the SHE management systems of contractor companies that offer their services to the petrochemical and chemical industry. The SCC scheme is owned and managed by the Central Committee of Experts. This body is made up of representatives of associations of both client and contractor companies. All logistical and technical issues regarding the scheme are coordinated by the 'Organisation for Cooperation on Safety'; in Dutch: Stichting Samenwerken Voor Veiligheid (SSVV) based in Rotterdam.

The SCC scheme is a voluntary scheme based on market mechanisms. Contracting parties can demand the SCC scheme from their suppliers. If, however, a supplier refuses to introduce the SCC scheme in his company he might well be soon out of business for this specific purchaser.

According to the Organisation for Cooperation on Safety, commissioning parties in the chemical industry found that a steadily growing amount of work on their premises was outsourced to third parties, like contractors for construction work, maintenance, etc. This development is continuing until today. Allowing workers from other enterprises to enter the high risk working environments of a commissioning party opts for a new strategy to control the level of safety of all workers (internal and external). The chemical industry was worried about the major differences between the safety performances of its

---

([8]) SHE = Safety, health and environment.

own personnel compared to personnel from third parties, such as contractors working on its premises. Therefore, the SCC scheme was introduced for these contractors to uphold the contractor's performance on worker's safety and health and environmental protection.

The aim of the scheme is more uniformity in SHE management systems and more continuous improvement of SHE performance within contractors' enterprises working on commissions for high risks industries such as the chemical industry. The SCC scheme has been introduced in The Netherlands, Belgium and Germany. Moreover, countries like Austria and Switzerland have lately started introducing the SCC scheme. In principle all branches can introduce the scheme. In practice companies working in high risk working environments in industry, installations and workplaces are more and more requiring from their subcontractors to introduce the SCC scheme. One must think of the following branches: petrochemical industry, offshore industry, dredging industry, railways, construction.

An important element of the scheme is the requirement for SCC-certified enterprises to demonstrate clearly that their personnel has received the obligatory SHE training. For this purpose a uniform national safety passport has been introduced in which all accepted and necessary safety training can be written down. More than 200 000 copies of this national safety passport have been issued to workers in SCC-certified companies. Just recently a uniform passport has been issued for Belgium and The Netherlands.

The SCC scheme consists of a list of questions that must be answered. Every question is explained and motivated in the SHE checklist contractors and some concrete verification points are mentioned that can demonstrate to the certification agency's if the criteria mentioned in a question can be met. Certification agency's that have an accreditation for SCC certification will audit the company.

There are two levels of certification.

SCC * (covers part of the list)

This assessment is directed towards the direct implementation of safety standards on the activities on the shop floor. This certificate is intended in principle for small companies (i.e. fewer than 35 employees, including temporary employees), which do not operate as main contractor.

SCC ** (covers the entire list)

In addition to the assessment described under SCC *, the company's SHE structures are also assessed. This certificate is intended in principle for companies with 35 or more employees, including temporary workers, and for small companies that operate as a main contractor.

Certification procedure

Each contractor working with a SHE management system in line with the SCC scheme, may request a certification agency for certification in accordance with the procedure defined and must be allowed access to this certification.

After the certification agency has received relevant company information from the contractor, a formal proposal shall be made regarding the 'evaluation' for certification and the subsequent periodic audits. An audit can only be carried out if the contractor's relevant SHE management system has been in operation for at least three months.

The evaluation follows three steps:

1. Documents

The auditor concerned shall after receipt, assess the documents, pertaining to the SHE management system.

2. Evaluation

The auditor discusses the questions with the appropriate responsible employees, coordinators and partners from the contractors.

3. Project visits

As a check on the document review and the interviews a number of work sites are to be visited.

Extension of the certificate

The SCC certificate is valid for a three-year period. Its extension is dependent on positive results of the audits, which are performed on a periodic basis (once per year minimum).

These evaluations are based on an audit plan, set up by the auditor during the initial evaluation. During such evaluations the SCC certification norm in force during the initial audit will apply.

This procedure must ensure that all the relevant aspects of the contractor's SHE management system are audited at least once during this three-year period. During the periodic audits it must be verified that the accident statistics are maintained on an annual basis.

The certification agency shall inform the company at least seven days beforehand of the intended audit. The audit must cover the entire period since the last audit. If the auditor finds during the audit that the situation does not comply with the SCC scheme, he/she will state this in the report. The company must in that case propose appropriate corrective measures to the certification agency and agree on a time period during which these corrective measures will be implemented. Should the corrective measures not have been implemented within the time period specified (maximum three months), then the SCC certificate must be suspended pending further investigation.

Suspension, withdrawal or annulment of the certificate

The certification agency may suspend, withdraw or annul a SCC certificate at any moment during the three-year certification period. The certificate may be suspended if the contractor fails to carry out corrective measures within the time period specified (maximum of three months), or if the logo or sign of the certification agency has been misused.

Costs for certification

Three elements influence the amount of costs involved for obtaining the SCC certificate:

1. preparatory costs: the company has to change its technical and administrative systems to comply with the SCC scheme; apart from these internal costs, external costs might arise for consultancy;
2. training costs: the SCC scheme demands obligatory safety training of personnel; these training programmes are uniform in their learning objectives and should be concluded with individual certificates;
3. certification costs: personal certification and auditing of the SCC scheme on company level brings along costs for diploma's and the auditing activities of the certifying authorities.

According to the Organisation for Cooperation on Safety the total out-of-pocket costs can vary between some thousands of euros to tens of thousands of euros depending on the initial state of the company's SHE management system. It is hard to describe the exact amount of costs involved. If apart from out-of-pocket costs, like described above, also lost time hours costs would be included the situation becomes even more complex.

Organisation of the scheme

The total SCC scheme is under the jurisdiction of the 'Organisation for Cooperation on Safety' (in Dutch: Stichting Samenwerken Voor Veiligheid = SSVV). A number of sectors are represented in this foundation. The foundation owns all rights to the scheme and the copyright of the logo. The Central Committee of Experts, operating as the executive body on behalf of the foundation, in fact owns and manages the scheme and monitors the quality.

The Central Committee of Experts consists of representatives from associations of both client and contractor companies. There is an equal balance in the amount of those representatives.

The Dutch Council for Accreditation supervises that the established procedures are followed.

Any complaints about the scheme or the way parties operate within this scheme, should in the first instance, be addressed to the certification agency. They will act according to the guidelines of the Council for Accreditation. In case this does not lead to a satisfactory solution, the complaint can be reported to the Council for Accreditation. The subsequent procedures will also involve the Central Committee of Experts.

6.3.2. Focus on occupational safety and health

The criteria of the SCC scheme are in general focused on the design, implementation and maintenance of a SHE management system on workers' safety and health and environmental protection. In order to obtain the SCC * (covers part of the list) all the following so-called 'must' criteria must be met positively. These criteria comprise:

- SHE (safety, health and environment) policy statement;
- appointment of S & H officer;
- risk inventory and evaluation;
- measures adopted following the risk inventory and evaluation;
- personal protective equipment;
- vocational training;
- SHE training;
- in-house SHE information and instruction;
- safety training for operational staff;
- safety training for operational supervisors;
- record in personal safety log;
- SHE meetings with operational staff;
- safety instructions, rules and regulations;
- periodic workplace inspections;
- following-up points for action;
- affiliation to occupational healthcare service;
- procedure for periodic medical examinations;
- medical examination for specific jobs;
- system for periodic inspection of equipment;
- registration of inspected equipment;
- identification of inspected equipment;
- procedure for reporting accidents and incidents;
- procedure for investing accidents and incidents;

and from 1 January 2003
- Training requirements for high risk jobs.

A point score is not required at this level. The verification may therefore be limited to the criteria above. Besides assessment of the SHE management system, the accident statistics must be taken into consideration. For this purpose the number of accidents involving absence per 1 000 000 man-hours work is utilised, expressed as an accident frequency index:

IF = number of accidents involving absence x 1 000 000 divided by number of hours worked.

Accidents involving absence must be included for all employee activities for which an SCC certificate has been applied for, including temporary staff. If the company's accident frequency index during the past three years has been greater than 40, no certificate may be issued. After the certificate has been obtained, full recertification for a new period of three years is subject to a 20 % improvement after a period of three years if the IF is between 25 and 40. The accident statistics must be verified during the audit. Also the average length of absence must be stated.

In order to obtain the SCC ** (covers the entire list) all the following so-called 'must' criteria must be met positively. These criteria comprise:

- all above-mentioned criteria for SCC *, plus:
- duties of supervisory staff;
- SHE workplace inspections;
- presence of SHE action plan;
- review of SHE action plan;
- SHE consultation at all levels;
- SHE rules and regulations;
- kick-off meetings with contractors;

and from 1 January 2003

- training requirements for high-risk jobs.

Besides these 'must' criteria, a point score of 110 must be obtained for the remaining questions in the SCC questionnaire. The requirements on the accident frequency scores are similar to SCC * certification.

6.3.3. Current use

The Organisation for Cooperation on Safety states that until the year 2000 around 7 000 SCC certificates have been issued. Every year an average of 1 500 new certificates is awarded. The SCC scheme is a well-known and respected certification scheme. A license agreement has been established with Belgium where also SCC certificates are now being awarded. The same developments are under way in Germany where also German suppliers have an ambition to be certified with the SCC scheme, especially when working on commissions from Dutch companies.

Many consultancy and training firms are assisting the enterprises that are preparing for their SCC certification. The SCC scheme has ignited an expanding investment in health, safety and environmental issues. A rough calculation by the Organisation for Cooperation on Safety indicated that since 1994 approximately EUR 1 billion must have been invested due to SCC certification.

A website has been launched (), both in Dutch and English. The website attracts a monthly amount of approximately 25 000 visitors. In future free downloadable texts will be supplied through the website.

6.3.4. Experiences

The Organisation for Cooperation on Safety intends to evaluate the effectiveness of the SCC scheme in close collaboration with the Technical University of Delft and TNO Work and Employment. An earlier evaluation (NIA TNO, 1998. See also section 'Suppliers' experiences) showed that SCC-certified companies realised a notable drop in accident rates.

Purchasers' experiences

With purchaser we mean the client company mostly in high-risk industries that contracts other companies for work on its premises. When a contractor company possesses a SCC certificate it has at least a basic, adequate, functioning SHE management system. For the purchaser making use of the services of an SCC-certified supplier the following advantages are obvious.

- A structure for the control of contractor-safety is available.
- Contractors can take their own responsibility for the implementation of a SHE management system.
- The overall quality of the work will improve so there is less lost-time.
- Safety audits are no longer necessary.

'Client companies not working in high-risk industries are also requiring SCC certification from their contractors.'

Eugène Hillen, director of the Organisation for Cooperation on Safety

SCC certification has confronted the client companies with the dilemma that sometimes their own personnel are less qualified than the SCC-certified contractor's personnel.

SCC certification has confronted the client companies with the dilemma that sometimes their own personnel is less qualified than the SCC-certified contractor's personnel. The Organisation for Cooperation of Safety is worried about this development that is possibly also caused by the unmotivated demand on SCC certification from client companies.

The Dutch employer organisation VNO-NCW is also worried about this development: 'SCC is rather expensive, especially for small and medium-sized companies, and in particular in cases in which the contractors have to meet the SCC requirements although they do not work in high-risk areas (for example window cleaners or gardeners)'.

Suppliers' experiences

With suppliers in this case we mean the contractor companies who have obtained SCC certification. For the supplier obtaining the SCC certificate the following advantages are obvious.

- The company qualifies for commissions with those purchasers who make an SCC certificate an obligatory condition. With respect to such purchasers there is no competition from contractors that are uncertified.
- It is no longer necessary for suppliers to focus on the various SHE questionnaires from client companies, allowing a structured approach to their own SHE management system.
- Auditing is done, in line with quality audits (ISO 9000), by an independent third party.

Some complaints are heard from contractor companies regarding the two major changes in the SCC scheme (1997 and 2000) with more severe verification criteria and a sterner accident frequency rate. Also the arbitrary requirement on SCC certification of low-risk client companies frustrates some contractor companies.

The Organisation for Cooperation of Safety is worried about this development that is possibly also caused by the unmotivated demand on SCC certification from client companies.

In an evaluation study (Cost/Benefits of OSH certification, NIA TNO, 1998) data of 77 SCC companies (suppliers) have been collected. In general these companies could quantify the costs for the certification. It appeared that the certification costs per employee were higher for smaller companies and also that in some sectors (e.g. construction) the costs were higher. It also appeared to be more difficult to quantify the benefits of the SCC certificate. However, two thirds of these companies were positive in their qualitative judgement on having acquired and worked with the SCC certificate, one third was neutral in their judgement, and only one company negative. Various advantages were expressed: acquiring contracts, decreased sickness absenteeism, less accidents, increased motivation of employees, efficiency improvements, market image of company, transparency in liabilities. Also 'critical' remarks were expressed: SCC is a voluntary scheme, however companies may feel forced to apply for the certificate to be able to operate in their market, the advantage of no competition from uncertified contractors may disappear as more companies acquire the certificate, (the possibility of) suspension, withdrawal or annulment of the certificate may damage business operations, some companies see a trend towards commercialisation of the certificate and along with this an 'inflation' of the SHE focus.

6.3.5. Impression of effectiveness and scale of application

As for society at large, indications are that the SCC certificate has the following advantages:

- less lost-time and incapacity for work owing to accidents at work;
- reduced risk of calamities.

The SCC scheme has developed a status in the Netherlands that can be compared with ISO standards.

The use of the SCC scheme is not any longer limited only to the petrochemical industry where it originated, but has widened also to branches like construction and metal industry.

Probably due to the widespread and still increasing use of SCC, social partner organisations in the Netherlands, employers as well as employee organisations take an interest in the SCC developments.

The Dutch trade union organisation 'FNV Bondgenoten' advocates an SCC scheme that in order to be effective, is supported at national level and has a 'strong' SHE focus.

Employer organisation VNO-NCW states that: 'SCC is the best possibility for the assessment of safety management that we have at this moment. However, it does not combine the maintenance of a safety and health system and the control and assessment. SCC is not a guarantee for safety; it can only function if the principal (purchaser) creates the right conditions in which the contractor

'The SCC certificate should, in our opinion, be developed into a real Dutch "poldercertificate". No longer a private affair of committees of experts of the (petro)chemical industry, but supported on a national level by employers and employee

organisations, possibly also the government. In this way we believe that the SCC certificate would have a better pay off and avoid becoming a piece of paper. Moreover, it would also prevent the fact that employers are using the SCC certificate to shift of their own responsibility in safety and health to their certified workers.'

The Dutch trade union organisation 'FNV Bondgenoten'

(supplier) can comply with the safety requirements'. According to the employers organisation attention has also to be paid to the fact that, 'SCC and safety and health management systems don't fully overlap each other. On the one hand SCC includes environmental aspects; on the other hand safety and health management systems include not only safety but also occupational health aspects. Contractors don't want to be confronted with the consequences of two different requirements: the one company requiring a SCC, the other company requiring a detailed management system'.

These statements do indicate that the social partner organisations in the Netherlands support the use of the SCC scheme, although they show hesitation on some points. The two organisations also agree that possibilities for further improvements should be explored.

The Central Committee of Experts has recently developed a quality manual. This manual allows all certification agencies to obtain the same information on procedures, forms and model contracts.

Three versions of the SCC scheme have been produced. The latest version was issued in March 2000.

Accreditation board system in the Netherlands

In many areas of commerce and industry it is usual for products, systems, processes, services or individuals to be certified as meeting certain required standards. In the Netherlands the official 'Accreditation Board' often makes use of the private accreditation system and certification. Certification has become a common instrument in the area of occupational safety and health. It is considered an important tool for a more effective policy of safety and health at work. The system is an entirely private one that nevertheless enables products, systems, etc. to be tested against legal standards where this is desired.

The Accreditation Board system comprises two levels. The board does not perform certification work itself, but checks that certification bodies possess the requisite independence, competence and reliability to do this work. To that end, the certification body must use a certification scheme which stipulates the standards which the product or service seeking certification must satisfy and the test procedures to be followed. The board recognises ('accredits') establishments that meet these standards.

A feature of the Accreditation Board system is that interested parties join together to form a Committee of Experts. They are jointly responsible for drafting and administering a scheme. As regards accreditation, this means that they must, on the basis of one of the European standards from the 45000 series, devise a scheme of accreditation for the certification process which the Accreditation Board then follows in laying down rules for certification bodies and supervising their work. As regards certification, interested parties in the Committee of Experts ensure that (statutory or other) standards are translated into requirements that can be enforced and quantified. In this way independent and expert certification bodies can issue certificates, based on a standard, which prove that the necessary requirements are met. As interested parties administer these schemes, their practical value is assured. Independent certification bodies are responsible for operational implementation. Certification bodies regularly check and re-check whether those concerned are complying with the requirements of the certificate. The Accreditation Board makes sure that certification bodies meet the standards required of them.

In the area of occupational safety and health the certification can be divided in three areas: product certificates, systems certificates and professional skill certificates. In all three areas there exist certificates that have been set up by the public authorities/government as there is a mandatory legal obligation. But in all three areas there also exist voluntary certification schemes. This means that a certification system has been initiated and set up by an interest group. These schemes can include existing legal requirements, but they also can deal with issues for which there exist no direct regulatory requirements.

Some 30 voluntary certification schemes have been introduced so far. The SCC scheme is a well-known example. The government considers it important that this development should be pursued further, so that compliance with statutory occupational safety and health obligations under the Working Conditions Act (ArboWet) becomes firmly enshrined in all sectors of industry and in company policy. In those sectors where a relatively large number of occupational safety and health certificates are issued, the Labour Inspectorate will have alternative ways of conducting its inspection work. Its duties will certainly not cease because its supervisory remit requires constant and adequate monitoring of conditions in the various sectors of industry. In this way the government is endorsing the view of the Social and Economic Council (SER) that certification must not replace the work of the Labour Inspectorate.

6.3.6 Further information

Further information on the SCC scheme can be obtained from:

The Netherlands: Central Committee of Experts (SCC), PO Box 443, 2260 AK Leidschendam. Tel. (31-70) 301 08 98; fax (31-70) 301 08 92; Internet: http://www.ssvv.nl; e-mail:ssvv@box.nl

Belgium: Secretariat Executive Committee of Experts (SCC), c/o Provincial Safety Institute, Jezusstraat 28–30, B-2000 Antwerp. Tel. (32-3) 203 42 00; fax (32-3) 203 42 50; e-mail: doc.centre@pvia.be

Germany: DGMK, Attn. Mr B. R. Altmann, Kapstadtring 2, D-22297 Hamburg. Tel. (49-40) 63 90 04 31; fax (49-40) 63 90 07 36

Switzerland: Eidgenössisches Amt für Messwesen Schweizerische Akkreditierungsstelle, Attn. Mr J. P. Jaunin, Lindenweg 50, CH-3003 Bern-Wabern. Tel. (41-31) 323 35 28; fax (41-31) 323 35 10

Austria: OMV AG EP-I-UBS/Arbeitssicherheit,Attn. Mr F. Pawlowitsch, Protesser Strasse 40, A-2230 Gänserndorf. Tel. (43-2282) 35 00 20 90; fax (43-2282) 350 09 75

6.4 STIMULATING OSH PROCUREMENT — THE SAFETY PASSPORT SCHEME

- United Kingdom
- Client driven
- Safety passport
- Approved training package
- Approved training providers
- Increased safety awareness

6.4.1. Background

Texaco's UK Pembroke refinery has long stressed the importance of contractor safety and has been a pioneer in the UK's development and implementation of contractor training programmes. Texaco was one of the founding members of a national programme for client contractors that was first implemented on sites in South Wales in early 1993.

This case study case describes the formation and development of the Client/Contractor National Safety Group (CCNSG) passport training scheme and how Texaco's Pembroke plant is working with both the scheme and safety and health in general in relation to contractors.

Many clients are moving to use of contractors, often working in areas that are potentially hazardous, to supplement their own workforces. This increase in the use of contractors in certain industrial sectors provided the impetus for developing ideas to improve accident rates. Contractor safety training was one of these.

It came from the general concern about the standard and knowledge of new starters at the sites. Some contractors in performing their work, travel from client to client. They commented that there were no common safety rules between different sites. Sometimes site inductions gave contradictory information whilst many wasted time by duplicating information.

To resolve this problem, owners of major hazard plants, their key contractors and specialist trainers got together to develop a basic safety course that was common to them all, that outlined simple rules and responsibilities for both workers and supervisors.

The content of this course covers H & S awareness and gives a base level of safety assurance to owners and contractors alike.

A different presentation format was devised involving open discussion between class members to share experiences and resolve problems. It requires those trained to reach a certain level by examination and those passing the test are awarded a passport. Supervisors are given additional modules relating to their responsibilities, and are examined too.

The scheme was developed in West Wales and training began in late 1992.

In 1995 a steering group was formed called the 'Client Contractor National Safety Group'. The role of the CCNSG Steering Group was to:

- drive and promote the scheme;
- review and develop the course contents;
- approve the training providers;
- set standards and maintain quality control over training providers;
- give advice to new client groups and others interested in the scheme.

Safety Train, a South Wales training provider, helped design and pilot the first course. The training package further developed by Safety Train is now compulsory for training providers joining the CCNSG passport training scheme.

As a result of the success of the CCNSG scheme, a non-profit-making company, the Safety Pass Alliance, has been set up to give access to other interested industrial sectors to variations of the existing scheme and the existing training provider network. The Safety Pass Alliance provides an alliance between clients, national training organisations and training providers. The training providers are quality audited and have a proven record in the design and delivery of safety passport training. These training providers are committed to provide the nationally recognised standard of safety and health training and assurance.

Whichever way you look at it, accidents cost us — not just in human terms of pain and suffering, but in such things as lost production and damaged equipment.

From the video: Safety passport training

6.4.2. Focus on occupational safety and health

The training course

The aim of the safety and health awareness training course is to ensure that, any contractor working for a participating client shall have a basic knowledge of safety and health. They should therefore, after appropriate site induction, work on-site more safely and with lower risk to themselves and others.

The CCNSG safety passport training course which has now been adopted nationwide is a two-day course taught to an agreed syllabus covering 10 modules.

1. Introduction to safety and health law and permit to work systems
2. Safe working practices

> *This safety and health training must not be seen as in any way relieving employers of their duties under current safety and health legislation, and is not seen as a replacement for adequate induction at site.*
>
> From the information material for scheme providers

3. Safe access and egress
4. Accident and first aid procedures
5. Fire precautions and procedures
6. COSHH and personal protective equipment (PPE)
7. Manual handling
8. Noise
9. Working with cranes and heavy equipment
10. Excavations

After each module or at the end of each day there is a test using multiple choice questions. The results from these tests add up to a final score. All candidates must answer the 100 questions and attain an 80 % pass mark before they are issued with a plasticised photographic pass. The safety passport is valid for three years after which revalidation can be achieved by attending a refresher course.

Some training providers have also published small booklets containing the key facts from the 10 modules of the training course.

The refresher course is a one day course which offers a re-cap of the 10 modules from the two-day course, and emphasises any revisions in legislation during the last three years. The refresher course can be given by any training provider, not necessarily the one who offered the first course.

The training courses involve a significant amount of trainee participation and the participants' practical experience is widely used in the discussions. Training focus is as much on stimulating safety awareness and safety culture as solely on knowledge-transfer. Consequently the courses teach people to go further than what is specifically required by regulation and not to compromise safety at any time.

Supervisors are required to attend an additional day, which highlights:

- the role of the supervisor;
- planning for safety and health;
- incident investigation;
- communication/presentation skills;
- risk assessment;
- safety monitoring.

The supervisors' course is more intensive and participative and follows a training package designed by GSS Personnel Services Ltd.

The maximum class size is 16 for the two-day training course and the refresher course and 10 for the supervisor course.

Training providers

Training is given by approved training providers. They are recommended by client groups, vetted by ECITB and approved by the CCNSG. They have their own national steering group and executive that report to the CCNSG. All approved training providers are audited annually by an independent auditor.

The instructors all have site experience and also have to attend the course themselves before they start training.

Contractor safety at Texaco

At Texaco's Pembroke plant it is a requirement for all contractors' hourly paid personnel and field supervision to show proof of having successfully completed the CCNSG safety passport training course.

On site there is a commercial group involved with contract work. New contractors fill in a questionnaire, which is scrutinised by key professionals including the safety advisor, to see if the potential contractor meets the required high quality, safety and health standards.

Safety and health is crucial, and as a result, contractors who do not have adequate safety management systems will not be approved, even though their costs may be attractive. Only if safety is acceptable are they approved to bid.

Some of the parameters included in the assessment of the contractor are:

- written safety policy;
- assessment of chemicals;
- accident performance;
- improvement notices from HSE;
- drugs and drink policy;
- references.

Contractor performance is monitored regularly by audits and contractors are rated upon conclusion of the contract.

Texaco has a close relationship with contractors and works with them continuously to improve on safety and health issues. Contractors attend monthly safety committee meetings and a number of proactive actions like audits, safety talks and preparation of safety plans are reviewed. Contractors also have to review their own accidents to identify and rectify trends to prevent recurrence.

At the contractors safety meeting, Texaco compares their performance using graphs. This enables them to measure their own performance against that of their peers, and to develop plans to improve. In this way, Texaco is helping to develop their safety culture.

Up to two years ago, staff and contractor accident rates were shown separately, but now they are combined and reported together. This has made a clear statement that the same rules apply for staff and contractors.

The following chart documents Pembroke's progress in reducing the combined lost time accident rate for employees and contractors from 1994 through 1998.

'If you can't do it safely, don't do it.'

Message passed at the training courses

'The only way to keep a contract with Texaco is to follow the rules.'

Bob Chesmer, Safety Advisor at Texaco

'We are trying to get through to the Rambo's and the don't knows.'

Bob Chesmer about the purpose of the training course

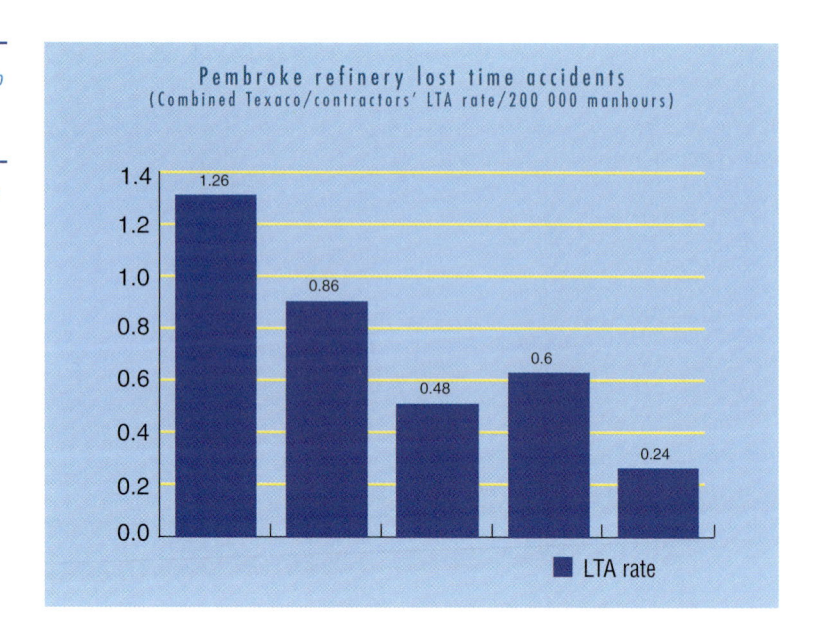

Pembroke refinery lost time accidents
(Combined Texaco/contractors' LTA rate/200 000 manhours)

Bar chart values: 1.26, 0.86, 0.48, 0.6, 0.24 — LTA rate

The safety principles applied at Texaco Pembroke plant are also communicated in booklets broken down into sections that are suitable for tool-box talks. One booklet is aimed at the operators and one at the supervisors.

The safety advisor from Texaco has been involved in both the creation and development of the CCNSG safety passport scheme and the evolution of the safety pass alliance scheme into other industrial sectors. Thus the experience with contractor safety and health from the Pembroke plant has been utilised.

6.4.3. Current use of scheme

The passport training scheme was originally intended for the engineering/construction industry but other industrial sectors have shown interest, and schemes have been developed for them by the safety pass alliance.

The passport training scheme has only been minimally advertised and has largely grown by word of mouth since 1993. The number of passport holders was 30 000 in 1997, 60 000 in 1998 and 114 000 in 1999. In 1999 it was used by more than 120 individual companies.

The number of training providers throughout the country is currently more than 70 with the CCNSG receiving 5 to 10 applications from potential training providers every week.

The passport training scheme is developed in all areas of the UK and the goal is now to spread it into other industrial sectors through the safety pass alliance. New sector training schemes will share common principles but will be sector-specific. Typically the two-day course will include 'the core day' followed by sector-specific modules.

Ireland is very interested in the scheme and next step will be European development.

The course fee is paid by the contractor and varies somewhat among the training providers. In general the fee is in the range of GBP 35 to 45 per day for the two-day/refresher course and GBP 120 to 135 for the supervisor course.

6.4.4. Experiences

Evaluation by HSE

The Safety and Health Executive took the initiative to evaluate the scheme in 1998/1999 because it was in use by so many major clients, and therefore commissioned a report from an external consultant ([9]).

According to the report, the passport scheme has fulfilled the original intentions of its sponsors. Net savings are thought to have been produced by reduced induction training and fewer accidents to individuals. Furthermore the scheme has, in general, contributed to safety culture both in the engineering construction and construction industries. The report concluded that 'most importantly, the scheme represents an outstanding example of large firms passing on their standards to smaller firms and their employees'. What the HSE report also emphasised was the courses' seeming ability to sensitise workers to safety and health matters in a way they can accept, so producing a long-term effect.

The underlying question asked was if the scheme should be mandatory.

HSE has since taken the view that it should remain a client-led initiative.

Texaco's safety advisor's experience

Texaco has noticed a significant change in the contractor's safety culture. When asked, following a shutdown where the accident rate had been cut by half, the contractors themselves considered the scheme to be the biggest single contributor to the improvement. Reports back to the CCNSG suggest similar safety and health improvements at other sites.

A reduction in accident and incidents rates at the Pembroke plant is considered likely to be a result of the increased safety awareness.

'A spin-off which I did not expect, was a cultural change at Texaco – contractors became more aware of their responsibilities.'

Bob Chesmer, Safety Advisor, Texaco

Training provider's experience

The results from a scheme survey sent out to 800 course participants showed that out of the 784 answers, 87 % found the course worth attending and 84 % found the time well spent.

Safety Train considers the development of the training package at the request of the client as the key to the success. The syllabus is not written by academics containing what they think industry wants. The training package actually represents the needs of the client group. Safety Train has also had feedback from clients saying that contract employees ask questions, which reflect an increased safety and health awareness at the induction courses that they have never asked before.

([9]) Evaluation of the Client/Contractor National Safety Group (CCNSG) passport training scheme by John Rimington, HSE 1999.

The schemes continuous development is discussed at the training providers' forum. Although the forums' main function is to assist newcomers to the scheme, the training providers sit together and discuss improvements even though they are competitors.

6.4.5. Impression of the effectiveness and scale of application

The CCNSG passport training scheme definitely seems to be a success within the engineering construction industry for which it was developed. According to the Safety Pass Alliance, the scheme supports a reduction in accident rates, increased safety awareness contributing to higher standards of safety performance. It provides better understanding of roles and responsibilities, familiarity with legal requirements and reduced on-site induction which can be revised to deal with key issues only resulting in quicker site mobilisation. These statements are also confirmed by the HSE evaluation.

There is no doubt that the passport scheme can be applicable in other industries as well. The HSE evaluation report concludes that the idea of client firms requiring contractors to complete safety awareness training as a condition of doing business can be useful in many other sectors, especially those using contractors extensively in potentially hazardous activities. The challenge, which will be met by the Safety Pass Alliance, will be to develop a training package to suit their special needs, sharing a common core.

The most obvious potential client groups are local authorities, docks, airports, food, rail, leisure, health, water and petroleum retail industries.

Identified by John Rimington in the HSE evaluation report

6.4.6. Further information

Additional information on the Client/Contractor National Safety Group (CCNSG) passport training scheme can be obtained from John Cushing at the Engineering Construction Industry Training Board. Tel. (44-1923) 26 00 00

Further information on safety passport training for other industrial sectors can be obtained from a Safety Pass Alliance Director at one of the three UK centres: North-West England. Tel. (44-1619) 26 95 10; Midlands, Tel. (44-1926) 81 33 56; South Wales, Tel. (44-1646) 60 00 62

6.5 STIMULATING OSH PROCUREMENT — BIGANOS EIG

- France
- Concept of subcontractor partnership
- Economic interest grouping
- Outside workers
- Paper industry

6.5.1. Background

This case is about the way the firm Smurfit — Cellulose du Pin (SCP), producer of 500 000 tonnes of packaging paper, located at Biganos in south-western France, manages its procurements and safety through an economic interest grouping (EIG) named the Biganos EIG.

For some years now, SCP has, like many industrial firms, focused on its core business and used subcontractors to perform maintenance of its installations. The average annual maintenance budget is around FRF 125 million, including FRF 70 million for subcontracting by approximately 70 firms, half of which are constantly present on the site. With a staff of over 500 direct employees and around 200 outside staff present daily as permanent or occasional subcontractors, SCP is faced directly with the problem of co-activity and its adverse consequences for the organisation of occupational safety.

A concept of proactive innovation, going beyond mere application of the regulatory texts, showing that safety and well-being in the workplace are in no way contrary to the economic efficiency necessary for satisfactory operation of the enterprise.

In the field of occupational safety and health SCP has a well-established culture in which personal well-being in the workplace is an essential value, considered as a factor of quality and progress. The objective of zero accidents on the Biganos site is accordingly stated clearly.

The issue: SCP, which has a proactive approach to occupational safety, made great efforts at the end of the 1980s to improve its performance in this field. At SCP, occupational safety is one of the essential factors of the total quality desired by any industrial firm.

This policy, which had positive results for the SCP employees, had however no effect on the employees of the subcontractors. The two populations of employees worked under different systems on the same site, and SCP therefore took measures to reduce the observed differences. To achieve this, outside companies were no longer allowed to operate without safety supervision.

These companies, with multiple skills, are of very different sizes. They may be local small and medium-sized enterprises or large groups. A common feature of these subcontractors is that they have personnel assigned permanently to the site. Personnel which is often very far away from the parent company. The permanently assigned staff consists of approximately 120 employees, to which should be added 80 temporary workers in peak periods. Some of the permanent staff has been present for many years (up to 6 to 9 years). This personnel performs maintenance tasks (lubrication/lighting), cleaning, fire protection, guard services, etc.

Objective: SCP expressed the desire to raise the occupational safety and health results of its subcontractors to the level of its own results via mutual management of safety aspects which are normally the responsibility of the subcontractors. More generally, the firm's objective was to integrate into an overall safety system those workers who are not its direct responsibility and whose employers are physically remote from the workplace of their employees.

> **Key points**
>
> - Permanent management of the co-activity of temporary workers and outside firms on a large industrial site requiring numerous varied skills for its maintenance operations, light and heavy, occasional and regular.
> - Permanent, light structure providing a personalised framework for outside personnel and enterprises, and follow-up and application of occupational safety and health regulations.

Means: To achieve this catch-up and pool energies to attain a mutual objective of quality and safety, a maintenance EIG (econonmic interest grouping) was set up in 1990. This voluntary grouping of the subcontracting firms present on the site ensures active solidarity between the various activities on behalf of the common customer, SCP. The concept of partnership is highlighted, and emphasis is placed on personal health in the workplace as a factor of quality and progress.

Membership of the EIG is voluntary and the EIG does not take the place of the subcontracting firm for commercial transactions. It works as a 'safety lock' through which all outside players have to go through.

6.5.2. Focus on occupational safety and health

Criteria: SCP took into account the following factors:

- subcontracting is called upon for hazardous jobs;
- increased use is made of outside players;
- these players have a poor knowledge of the site and its rules;
- there is interference between the outside players and production.

The prevention procedure should therefore be based on a strong partnership between the subcontracting firms and the customer firm SCP, which translated into setting up of the EIG.

Parameters: For its own personnel, SCP had, through a policy of training and promotion of awareness, brought the rate of accident frequency down from 22.7 to 7.9 and the severity rate down from 0.56 to 0.17 between 1987 and 1990.

These same factors were incorporated in the objectives of the EIG, with a view to reducing the rates for the subcontracting firms to make them finally equivalent to those of SCP.

6.5.3. Current use of the scheme

Scope of the system: The creation of this innovative management tool, the EIG, enables the client SCP to be a player in prevention. The EIG is a light structure serving as a framework for the subcontracting firms and their employees. It ensures coordination and integration at all levels of safety and health concerns in the stages of work preparation and performance and monitoring and follow-up of these same operations.

Functioning: The EIG groups together most of the subcontracting firms operating temporarily or permanently on the site.

The EIG has a permanent management employee and secretariat. One of the main roles of the manager is to regularly ensure strict compliance with the safety and health regulations in force. He has received a proxy from the subcontractor members of the EIG for this purpose. The manager is empowered to stop the work if he observes a failure to comply with the rules. Through his presence on the site and his powers, he relieves the subcontracting employers of their criminal liability.

The EIG is financed by a contribution paid by its members, amounting to 2 % of the total value of services performed by the subcontractor on behalf of SCP.

The EIG is a framework structure for the subcontracting firms. It was very well positioned to draw up a set of general safety and health requirements specific to the paper industry and the Biganos site. This document enables the firms involved to be informed of customs and practices on the site. It is supplied to all new firms that become members of the grouping.

For each contract signed with the contracting firm a preliminary joint inspection for risk analysis is performed with the subcontractor. This analysis involves thinking in which the contracting firm, the subcontractor and the EIG are involved. Collective and personal protective systems, risks at the work station, the required authorisations and qualifications and the appropriate equipment and tooling necessary to accomplish the assignment are defined during this inspection. As coordinator, the EIG takes part for each contract in working out a prevention plan.

The EIG also welcomes and follows up the personnel. An introduction to safety matters is provided systematically for each player. During this welcome interview, the Biganos site and the plant rules are outlined and a booklet entitled 'General safety instructions' is handed out. By registering each worker and giving him a personal identification card, the EIG makes sure that his training and equipment are adequate to enable him to meet safety requirements. His occupational qualification, capability and compulsory authorisations are checked.

The EIG thus enables continuous follow-up of the players even though they are far from their parent firm. This management system ensures that the employee maintains his identity with regard to his firm; it is also required that his work clothes be identified with the name of his company.

Control of subcontracting firms: Each firm is evaluated quarterly by its 'customers' in the prime contracting firm. Evaluation is performed by the direct users of the services and includes numerous safety points. For each firm a rating sheet is established, with 10 criteria having four possible levels of satisfaction. These results, compiled in the form of a satisfaction index on an annual overall evaluation sheet, serve as a basis for the annual interview between the subcontractor and SCP.

This evaluation index is considered a fair, simple and reliable instrument. It is appreciated and its results are awaited by the subcontracting firms which then use them internally. Since its creation, constant progress has been observed for the index.

6.5.4. Experiences

Originality: It is fundamental to note that SCP is the only buyer but that several client departments within the firm call on subcontractors. These clients then have the supplier firms carry out work according to their needs. The centralising role of the EIG ensures the coherence of the system on the crucial point of occupational safety and health.

The proactive attitude of the client (prime contractor) should be noted, because it is the cornerstone for the success of this system combining economic results with positive results regarding occupational safety and health. The desire to intervene in this area can also be explained by a need to avoid too heavy a burden being placed on the enterprises. Recognising that safety should be handled by the firm and taking the matter in hand, the firm restricts reasons for intervention by the legislator.

Experience of buyers: This practice, which needed no additional financial resources to operate, is used by all buyers on the site for all products and services. Purchasing is managed at SCP by two departments, the purchasing department and the maintenance department; it is practised at various levels for the organisation of operations.

Occupational safety and health criteria weigh heavily in the decision-making process. For each contract, a selection criteria grid is established. These criteria are weighted; cost does not have the greatest weight, counting for 10, whereas the weight is 30 for site safety, preparation and work. In practice, moreover, at equal prices SCP gives preference to members of the EIG.

Firms were excluded from the EIG in the initial years – approximately 12 % — more for failure to comply with safety rules and lack of personnel management than for other reasons.

Experience of suppliers: Membership of the EIG does not discourage firms, and taking part in it is considered as a label recognising the quality of the services provided. Membership is part of a proactive approach by the firm. At the time of the creation of this EIG, 19 subcontracting firms became members, whereas the current number is approximately 35. Some subcontractors on a national scale are members of several EIGs.

One of the original features of this system lies in the fact that the subcontracting supplying firms finance the EIG. In return these suppliers gets a service which enables them to have their personnel work without worries on a remote, complex industrial site.

Membership of the EIG is considered a quality label in the area.

Mr G. Fabiani, FIG Director

6.5.5. Impression of effectiveness and scale of application

Industry makes an intensive use of subcontracting generating co-activity and its problems. The formula of the EIG avoids problems of cohabitation between different employee populations who have little knowledge of one another. The EIG promotes the structuring of safety on large industrial sites; its other advantage is to bring all available safety measures and regulations within range of small and medium-sized enterprises and their personnel.

Since its creation, 10 years ago now, the EIG has seen the number of occupational injuries fell by 75 % on the site. The frequency rate fell to 12/12.5 in 1999 (from 41 in 1990) and the severity rate was below 0.10 for 1999. By limiting dysfunctions due to safety and organisation, SCP also ensures improved availability of the industrial facilities on its site.

This system is transferable and it has already been replicated three times, — it is well known and it draws great interest. To introduce it, the management of the client firm needs strong determination and must clearly present the objectives to its personnel. The structure of the EIG is adaptable preferably to industrial sites performing continuous production and making extensive use of subcontracting. It can be adapted to high-tech industries as was the case when an EIG formed around the Blayais nuclear power plant. This EIG works in the same spirit on behalf of EDF (French Electricity Board) and its members are likewise local small and medium-sized enterprises.

6.5.6. Further information

Mr Gérard Fabiani, Manager, GIE Biganos Allée des Bruyères, F-33380 Biganos. Tel. (33) 557 70 61 70; fax (33)557 70 61 72; e-mail: gfabiani@aol.com

6.6 ETHICAL INVESTMENT — TRIODOS BANK

Triodos ⊛ Meerwaardefonds

- Netherlands
- Banking sector
- Ethical investment fund
- Procurement of stocks

Where more than money counts.

| About us | Triodos Bank Belgium | Triodos Bank Netherlands | Triodos Bank UK |

6.6.1. Background

Triodos Bank has distinguished itself since 1980 by its innovative and transparent approach to banking activities. It is a social bank combining the financing of social, cultural and environmental projects and businesses. It is lending to and investing in organisations and businesses bringing a positive contribution to society and environment. Among a comprehensive list of social and environmental concerns there is also the safety and health issue. Although the bank takes this criterion into account in its lending process, this case study will focus on one specific investment product of Triodos Bank, that is the MeerWaarde fund.

This case study describes how Triodos Bank integrates the safety and health criterion in its investment policy, why this criterion was integrated, and how companies react to it.

Triodos Bank is one of Europe's leading ethical banks. It was founded in 1980 in the Netherlands to finance a new generation of enterprises creating social added value and caring for the environment, and to give people new ways to save and invest ethically. Nowadays Triodos is an international bank with offices in Belgium, UK and The Netherlands. It belongs to national and international networks of financial institutions active in the social economy.

Triodos Bank strongly believes that social and environmental interests should be taken into account in economic decisions. Financial and economic aspects cannot be viewed in isolation from society as a whole. Therefore, Triodos Bank wants to be more than a mere financial instrument that is exerting a positive influence on the developments of which they are a part. Triodos Bank seeks to contribute to the social economy by investing in sustainable economic development, both socially and for the environment.

The bank offers a wide range of banking services including savings accounts for individuals, and current and investment accounts for social businesses, charities and groups. Triodos Bank has also set up various investment funds among those the MeerWaarde fund. It is a so-called ethical investment fund, that buys (sells) publicly traded common stocks on the basis of social, environmental and financial criteria. The MeerWaarde Fund is managed jointly by Triodos Bank and Delta Lloyd Asset Management. They have been working together since 1990 in investments based on social and environmental criteria. Their starting point was the conviction that it is possible to combine good returns on investment with a responsible use of natural resources by enterprises and institutions, which also have a distinctive social policy.

The added value investment fund (in Dutch: 'Meerwaarde Fonds') has been launched in May 1997 on the AEX (Amsterdam Stock Exchange). The fund invests in companies, which are able to demonstrate a more than average result on business ethics in relation with good financial performance. Selected companies and institutions are the ones, whose activities have a minimal impact on the environment and positive social effects. This may be either through their products or services, or a well-considered social and environmental policy. Both Triodos Bank and Delta Lloyd by accepting to manage an ethical fund, state that such investment philosophy will in the long term lead to market returns and will be a contribution to the well-being of the society.

> The purpose of the MeerWaarde fund is to provide a banking product which:
> - lives up to investors values;
> - opens a dialogue between investors and companies;
> - stimulates social and environmental performances without neglecting the financial performance;
> - promotes awareness about social and environmental responsibilities within the business community.

The investment selection is based on two sets of criteria, the so-called exclusion and the comparative criteria. Companies are excluded from the investment universe if their activities are harmful to people, animals and the environment. A typical list of ethical concerns of ethical funds might include 'alcohol production, factory farming, fur industry, animal testing, drugs, genetic modification, nuclear energy, tobacco, arms industry … child labour, dictatorial regimes, corruption …' ([10]). If the company fulfils the exclusion criteria, it is then screened on comparative criteria such as environmental management and policy, emissions,

---
[10] [Triodos Research, 1999 #139]

waste, social policy, working conditions, contribution to society, etc. Companies are compared and benchmarked on the basis of those comparative criteria. The 'best in class' (50 % best) companies of the same sector are included in the universe for ethical investment. There is, indeed, a third set of criteria, which are the financial criteria. It consists of the usual criteria used for investment decision. Screening and monitoring on social and environmental issues are carried out by Triodos Research, while Delta Lloyd does the financial screening and monitoring.

Public information, like annual accounts and information from interviews with companies is used in the research into sectors and enterprises. Also knowledge from third parties is used, like research institutes, branch organisations, environmental organisations, unions and authorities.

After internal discussion within Triodos research, an investment advice is sent to the companies concerned and to Delta Lloyd for the financial screening and portfolio management. Companies that have been investigated by the Triodos Research are monitored, so that relevant changes in social, environmental and financial fields can be taken into account. Studies in order to find the companies 'best in class' are repeated every three years. This can lead to changes in investment advice.

6.6.2. Focus on occupational safety and health

Safety and health is present throughout the whole screening process. Safety and health is considered by Triodos Bank as one very important criterion in its investment policy. Every company has the duty to provide good working conditions and a healthy and safe work environment to its employees. This is important for the well-being of its employees. Companies can be excluded from the investment universe because of their bad performances on the safety and health criterion. In the following paragraphs we describe the way Triodos Bank looks at occupational safety and health first through the exclusion criteria and then through the comparative ones.

Exclusion criteria

Triodos Bank considers the safety and health factor as indispensable for the creation of a sustainable and humane society. It states in the following three specific exclusion criteria:

- Working conditions
  companies that frequently and seriously fail to take measure to avoid unsafe or unhealthy working conditions;
- Breaches of environmental law
  companies that have caused serious damage to the environment or frequently and seriously breach environmental legislation;
- Breaches of legislation, codes of conduct and treaties
  companies that frequently and seriously breach labour legislation, other relevant legislation, codes of conducts or treaties.

Regarding safety and health, the minimum requirement for Dutch companies is the compliance with the Dutch occupational safety and health Act. In case of non-compliance with one or more of the above criteria, the company is excluded. Note that safety and health is only one aspect of the exclusion screening. In total, Triodos Bank looks at 33 exclusion criteria.

The comparative criteria

After the exclusion screening, which is the minimum requirement for Triodos Bank, the second round of screening takes place, the comparative criteria. In this set, safety and health plays an important role. The minimum requirement is not enough, any company should strive to go beyond it.

Triodos Bank looks at the following points:

- systems for monitoring safety and health at work;
- absence due to illness;
- staff turnover;
- accidents;
- security of employment;
- work climate/stress/overtime;
- facilities.

Companies are assessed on each of these criteria and are compared to each other. The above criteria are part of a larger list of criteria concerning social and environmental concerns.

Exclusion criteria ⟶ The company can be excluded from the investment universe because of non-respect of the minimum safety and health requirements.

Comparative criteria ⟶ The company can be left out of the investment universe because of its under-performance on safety and health criteria compared to its sector average.

6.6.3. Current use of scheme

The screening process is used for the MeerWaarde fund in order to define the investment universe. Delta Lloyd, who manages the fund, can invest only in this universe shaped by social and environmental concerns. It is what distinguishes ethical investment from regular investments. Through this process, Triodos Bank gets into dialogue with companies. This takes place through the examination of information, interview(s), sending advice to companies and feedback from the companies on the advice.

Triodos is considered as a pioneer bank in the Netherlands, but it is not an exceptional case in its approach to ethical investment. Financial institutions are more and more integrating ethical criteria and therefore safety and health criteria into their investment funds. To illustrate the growing concern about environmental matters within financial institutions, in the UK ethical investments have been multiplied by 7.14 in eight years (from GBP 280 million in 1990 to GBP 2 billion in 1998); in the same period the number of funds has risen from 18 to 24.

'Should companies apply the minimum level of safety and health required in each country or should companies apply the highest level required to all its branches?'

T. Thijssens, Research Analyst, Triodos Research

6.6.4. Experiences

Triodos researchers' experience

Applying criteria such as safety and health to investment policy is not always easy, although researchers have got a good insight and knowledge into the issue for each screened company. In order to do that the dialogue with the company is crucial. It helps to understand better the business and the organisation of the company.

Sometimes Triodos has no direct access to relevant information. For example the (Dutch) Labour Inspectorate, enforcing companies to comply with the Occupational Health and Safety Act, has a legal obligation to handle available information as confidential. Triodos has to find other sources of information in order to get complementary information on companies. The multi-source of information is at the core of Triodos' methodology. Researchers are in constant contact with third-party organisations in order to get several point of views, which are sometimes different. Sometimes, researchers are confronted by the unwillingness of some companies to disclose information. It entails at a negative weight in the screening. It makes the evaluation difficult because it is based on limited sources of information. A common problem the researchers are confronted with is a lack of consistency of information. It is particularly true on a global scale. International companies do not always provide information for the whole group. Safety and health regulation is not the same in every country. That leaves out the question if all companies should apply the minimum level of safety and health required in each country, or if companies should apply the highest level required to all its branches.

Triodos favours the second option but it is difficult to check. After the screening, Triodos benchmarks companies. It raises the problem of comparing information, which is sometimes very different.

Triodos appreciates initiatives such as global reporting initiative, in which there is a section on, because it makes information more comparable.

Triodos feels that companies take its enquiries seriously and the ethical investment movement in general. Once, a screened company has invited Triodos to discuss the way to report on and other issues in their annual report, the interview within the company is usually welcomed and appreciated. According to Triodos' researchers, there are differences among companies regarding the way they answer, from pure formality to real involvement. The best for the researchers would be to have a constant dialogue with companies, and feedback on the advice they send after screening.

Evaluation by companies

Companies interviewed have shown real enthusiasm regarding ethical investment. They appreciate that banks look at a broader range of criteria than pure financial ones.

Companies take the screening as an opportunity to have an objective point of view on their social and environmental performances. This also helps

---

'Every company has its own way of reporting on safety and health. We value companies that go beyond the minimum regulation requirement. We value proactive companies. It makes the benchmark between companies also more difficult.'

T. Thijssens, Research Analyst, Triodos Research

'It is important that external bodies acknowledge companies that take care of social and environmental concerns.'

R. Broekhuis, Wegener Arcade

them to understand how their activities and behaviours are perceived externally and it is important for the image and identity of the company and for the employee.

Companies interviewed for this report emphasised the importance of the dialogue with Triodos Bank. They now and then receive questionnaires for ethical investment screening. But having a direct contact with the researchers makes a difference. Because of that they take the screening more seriously. In general, they appreciate having the opportunity to give feedback on the advice before Triodos takes its final decision on the selection or exclusion of the company.

Companies are aware that Triodos gets information from third parties such as trade unions and NGOs. They find it important in order to check the information from the companies.

The way the advice is handled differs from company to company. Some disclose the information in their environmental report, others just inform the management team about the result of the screening. It often helps to improve the reporting on issues such as safety and health.

6.6.5. Impression of the effectiveness and scale of application

The MeerWaarde fund seems to be a success in terms of opening a dialogue with companies. Companies screened by Triodos value its advice and take the studies carried out by the bank seriously. They usually work on the weak points mentioned in the advice of Triodos and send feedback and/or follow up developments to Triodos. Such investigations from financial institutions have an influence on corporate image.

According to companies screened by Triodos, an ethical investment fund such as the MeerWaarde fund cannot in itself change the behaviour of corporate policy but contributes to making companies more aware of their responsibilities. Companies consider safety and health an important aspect of the 'ethical' behaviour.

6.6.6. Further information

More information about Triodos Bank can be obtained from Bas Rüter, Head of Saving and Investment Department in Triodos Bank. Tel. (31-30) 693 65 00

'Who would like to work with a company with a bad record on safety and health?'

R. Broekhuis, Wegener Arcade

'Third party information is important in order to keep an objective point of view on the company and to check what we are saying.'

L. van Aalten, Van Melle

European Agency for Safety and Health at Work

SYSTEMS AND PROGRAMMES

7.

GOVERNMENTAL PROCUREMENT INITIATIVES

7.1 STIMULATING OSH PROCUREMENT — THE GOOD NEIGHBOUR SCHEME: HSE

- United Kingdom
- OSH assistance to small companies
- Networking

7.1.1. Background

The UK Government, the Health and Safety Commission (HSC) and the Health and Safety Executive (HSE) are keen to promote occupational safety and health issues via the supply chain. Indeed, supply chain initiatives feature prominently in a joint government/HSC venture, 'Revitalising health and safety', which aims to inject new impetus into the UK safety and health system. This case study originates from the UK and describes a scheme to encourage organisations to share their expertise in managing safety and health with their contractors, suppliers, neighbouring organisations and the wider community.

The UK good neighbour scheme was launched by the Chairman of the Health and Safety Commission in 1997 during the European Week for Safety and Health. HSE's role is to facilitate local networks and self-sustaining initiatives. HSE currently promotes the good neighbour scheme via 'good neighbour forums' held throughout the UK. Forums are half-day events organised jointly by HSE and a partner (e.g. trade union, safety charity, employers' organisation). They provide an opportunity for good neighbours to tell their suppliers, contractors and others what they have been doing to manage safety and health, and what help they can offer. Previous forums have included representatives from industries as diverse as the nuclear power industry and local authorities. Good neighbour forums bring like-minded employers together, building links in the local community.

HSE is currently preparing a directory of good neighbours, which will soon be available on the HSE website. This will enable anyone interested in the scheme to access further information and contacts directly. HSE is also planning an evaluation of the good neighbour forums held to date to establish what impact they have had on safety and health management in participating firms, and how sustainable good neighbour partnerships are over time.

The principal aims of the good neighbour scheme are to:

> - encourage large firms to commit themselves to sharing their safety and health expertise and resources with contractors, suppliers and neighbouring firms;
> - encourage small firms to appreciate the benefits of working with organisations which have established good safety and health practices, and to take action to improve their own safety and health management;
> - foster a change in attitudes to safety and health and promote behaviour which will lead to improved performance.

In the search for quality, bigger firms are putting increasing emphasis on the safety and health capability of their suppliers, as well as their capacity to deliver the goods. Those who do not measure up as either contractors or as subcontractors will find themselves increasingly squeezed out of the supply chain ([1]).

As well as providing access to practical experience in managing safety and health, being a good neighbour by participating in the good neighbour scheme:

- helps employers to feel more confident that people they work with are aware of safety and health issues. Overlooking the safety and health performance of workers, contractors or suppliers can be expensive. There are potential losses — sometimes uninsured — in production time, key workers, products and equipment, not to mention possible legal proceedings;
- adds to employers' experience of managing safety and health, and could put them in a better position to contract for future work. In HSE's experience, more and more employers are recognising the potential knock-on effects of inadequate safety and health management. We are seeing a growing tendency for employers to ask those they work with about how they manage safety and health. Sometimes, safety and health issues are covered in contractual requirements;
- enhances an organisation's corporate reputation in the eyes of those it works with and others in the community. Reputation is now recognised as a key factor in keeping existing business and winning new work.

In favour of the scheme: Most firms, particularly large ones, have regard for the communities surrounding their gates, from which they draw their workforce. Some firms see their continued existence as bound up with the need to secure local support and tolerance. Involvement on a practical, or purely charitable level is quite common. Large firms often give discreet support to local business communities, and to smaller firms who often enough seek advice from them, in preference to official agencies. Some firms offer spare places on their in-house safety and health training courses; many give assistance to small

---
([1]) Managing Risk — Adding Value, (1998) HSE Books, ISBN 0-7176-1536-7

contracting firms who need to meet contractual requirements, particularly in relation to safety and health policies and risk assessments. There are sound business reasons for such strategies and initiatives, beyond simply fostering goodwill and promoting corporate reputation.

A key motivator is the need for firms to maintain their local supply bases, e.g. for trained and well-disciplined personnel and for contractors. And many employers now recognise that overlooking the safety and health performance of their workers, contractors or suppliers can be expensive. There are potential losses — sometimes uninsured — in production time, key workers, products and equipment, not to mention possible legal proceedings.

In practice, client companies have a vested interest in improving their suppliers' safety and health performance. Moreover, there is no doubt that client firms exercise considerable power and influence in business relationships. In safety and health terms, as with many other considerations, clients require others to meet their quality management standards. HSE research suggests that safety and health performance is frequently used to indicate the general management competence of contractors and suppliers, precisely because it is an aspect which is often neglected. Clients promote safety and health by exercising control based on their own knowledge and expertise. In effect, client firms wield a powerful 'carrot and stick' over those who seek to contract with them.

Good neighbours have the advantage of controlling what they contribute and how. Some will also receive HSE awards during annual European weeks for safety and health for their contribution to the scheme. With regard to the client–contractor relationship, the scheme fosters closer partnerships. Moreover, much of the knowledge acquired from a specific client–contractor good neighbour partnership, particularly if it relates to general safety and health management techniques, is likely to be of wider benefit to a supplier/contractor.

Against the scheme: Since participation in the good neighbour scheme is voluntary, firms cannot be forced to take part. Even with encouragement from a particular client, a contractor may choose to risk losing that client or seek work with others, rather than participate in the scheme. In addition, a participating contractor might not gain any recognition of improved performance outside of the client organisation. And, unless individual performance is targeted by the initiative, both client and contractor remain vulnerable to the actions of individual workers.

7.1.2. Focus on occupational safety and health

The HSC good neighbour scheme is entirely voluntary and focuses solely on occupational safety and health. However, there are schemes run by other UK organisations (including other government departments and employer representative organisations) which similarly exploit supply chain levers to promote different issues (e.g. environmental management, general business administration, etc).

Good neighbour initiatives can relate to any aspect of occupational safety and health: generic (e.g. risk assessment) or topic-focused (e.g. manual handling). However, there is the potential to facilitate greater awareness of social responsibilities by encouraging work with firms outside the supply chain, such as local schools and charities. This is an avenue that the HSE will be looking to explore in the future.

The HSC good neighbour scheme is entirely voluntary and focuses solely on occupational safety and health.

Examples of good neighbour activities, which have been shown to work well with firms of all sizes, are:

- seminars and face-to-face discussion, including invitations to attend in-house seminars and presentations;
- training events, including offering places on in-house courses and carrying out simulated emergency exercises;
- providing information to stimulate discussion, for example, distributing posters and leaflets, talking to school children;
- safety and health quizzes, such as hazard-spotting quizzes for on-site contractors, or team events in which local contractors or businesses can field teams;
- offers of safety and health expertise, e.g. in assisting firms in the same sector with risk assessments, involving safety and health representatives in monitoring contractors;
- offering on-site occupational health services to local companies.

7.1.3. Current use of the scheme

The good neighbour scheme is an HSC initiative, which applies throughout the UK. So far, good neighbour forums, the main vehicle for promoting the scheme, have been held in six locations around the country (Newcastle upon Tyne, Manchester, Rutland, Exeter, Glasgow and Cambridge). Each forum has involved around 120 people from a variety of sectors. Other good neighbours are recruited through participating firms and word-of-mouth. It is hoped that the good neighbours directory on the HSE website will help to extend the good neighbour network.

7.1.4. Experiences

Feedback from the good neighbour forums indicates that the vast majority of participating organisations and supplier/contractor delegates find the events worthwhile and that the principles behind the good neighbour scheme are valid. HSE is currently commissioning research to assess the longer term impacts of the forums.

HSE has generally found that there are many intermediary organisations keen to assist in organising good neighbour forums. Moreover, recruiting participating organisations is usually fairly straightforward.

7.1.5. Impression of effectiveness and scale of application

Although feedback from the good neighbour forums has generally been positive, it is difficult to comment on the effectiveness of the good neighbour scheme at the time of writing this report. HSE will get an impression of this as part of its evaluation of the forums. HSE will also be considering whether there are other ways, in addition to the forums and the directory, to promote the scheme. However, the scheme seems to be widely applicable across all sectors and size of company, because the principles behind it are equally generally relevant.

7.1.6. Further information

More information about the UK good neighbour scheme can be obtained from Andie Michael in the Strategy and Analytical Support Directorate of the Health and Safety Executive. Tel. (44-20) 77 17 64 88

7.2 BELGIAN POLICY REGARDING OSH IN PROCUREMENT

FEDERAAL MINISTERIE VAN TEWERKSTELLING EN ARBEID

MINISTERE FEDERAL DE L'EMPLOI ET DU TRAVAIL

7.2.1. Background

The structure of Belgian legislation in general and in the area of occupational safety and health in particular reflects its position between two distinct European cultures with respect to the formulation of regulations. On one hand the Latin approach, which is based more on compulsory rules, while the Anglo-Saxon approach is based on setting objectives and involves a more voluntary approach.

In order to deal pragmatically with the tensions between these two approaches in the area of occupational safety and health, Belgium established a statutory frame that lays down the objectives of the regulations together with ways to obtain these objectives. A number of compulsory procedures in the field of procurement have been established with the aim of controlling OSH risks in Belgian companies:

- the purchase of work equipment and protective equipment;
- the purchase of dangerous substances;
- working with contractors and third parties;
- employment agency work;
- OSH in public contracts.

These initiatives are explained in more detail hereafter.

- *Belgium*
- *Purchasing procedures for products, work equipment, and services*
- *Three green lights procedure*
- *OSH in public contracts*

Occupational safety and health in marketing and procurement

> *'Procurement, i.e. the promotion of the control of risks entering the company, is the social answer to the complexity and flexibility of workplaces and workers.'*
>
> Luc Van Hamme, director Labour Inspectorate

In Belgium in the field of procurement a number of compulsory procedures have been established to control OSH risks in companies. For some of these obligations such as the so-called 'three green lights' procedure for the purchase of work equipment and protective equipment there exist compliance indicators. These indicate an increase in the use of procurement procedures.

7.2.2. Focus on occupational safety and health

The purchase of work equipment and protective equipment

A Royal Decree on prevention in the area of OSH has been in force since 20 June 1975. In addition to some general principles of prevention, it also includes a specific procedure for the purchase of mechanical work equipment and collective and individual protective equipment. This specific procedure was set up because of the high accident rates with machines and problems with poor ergonomics design. Although the more recent European directives on work equipment and protective equipment did not contain these specific elements, the original Belgian compulsory procedures were nevertheless retained, implying that Belgian regulation on the issue goes beyond the minimum standards required by European directives.

The purchase procedure comprises three stages (also known as the 'three green lights').

- Employers must obtain the opinion of their Prevention and Protection at Work Service before any purchase of mechanical work equipment or collective or individual protective equipment. The service has to mark the orders as proof of being seen.
- Suppliers must provide a certificate stating that the requirements regarding safety and health indicated on the order form have been met.
- The Prevention and Protection at Work Service must confirm this upon delivery and issue a report of entry into use.

In the case of equipment with an EC marking, the procedure applies only in respect of those aspects that are not covered by the marking and of any special requirements.

The purchase of dangerous substances

In order to enable employers to carry out a proper risk evaluation on the issue of dangerous substances, they must have access to all relevant information. This includes all situations where dangerous substances are being processed. This particular information is usually only available from the supplier. Many of these products are not dangerous if used correctly under normal circumstances. European directives on product labelling cover only the intrinsic properties of the products. However some of the low-risk products may pose a serious risk under specific processing conditions and use situations.

In order to deal with this issue an Act has been adopted on 28 January 1999. This Act aims to ensure and promote the well-being of workers that deal with chemical substances and preparations. This Act on Dangerous Substances requires that suppliers disclose to employers all necessary information to enable them to fulfil their obligations regarding the well-being of workers.

> **Box 1: Belgian regulations regarding the prevention of occupational risks**
>
> Belgian regulations regarding the prevention of occupational risks place the following obligations on employers:
> - to set up a system of risk control based on a five-year global prevention plan which is implemented by an annual action plan;
> - to set up an Internal Prevention and Protection at Work Service within the company, based on size, sector and staffed by experts with specified educational level;
> - to set tasks which have to be fulfilled by the Prevention and Protection at Work Service;
> - to hire an external Prevention and Protection at Work Service when the necessary expertise is not available in the company itself.

Working with contractors and third parties

In Belgium, working with contractors and third parties is governed by the Act of 4 August 1996 on well-being at work. This Act identifies a number of elements to be taken care of. Companies that undertake work at the same place have to cooperate over the implementation of the measures to ensure health and safety of workers and also must coordinate their activities and exchange information. The fact of being present at a place where work is performed is enough for this regulation to apply.

The protection of well-being at work for the parties involved in a contract is ensured by a specific Act on contracts and well-being at work (principal organisations and contractors). This procedure involves three steps.

Stage 1: Obligation of precaution

Firstly, the principal organisations are obliged to reject companies or individuals from the tendering process if it is known that the latter is not concerned about the well-being of workers. Although no precise indication is given about how this should be done, it can for example be implemented by examining the performance of the companies concerned in this area in the annual report of their Internal Prevention and Protection at Work Service. Principal organisations may also require voluntary certification systems such as the contractors safety checklist or the Belgian safety criteria for contractors. More details about this are given in the case on Electrabel (to be found earlier in this report).

Stage 2: Contractual obligation

Secondly, principal organisations must conclude an agreement (contract) with the contractor (company or individual) stating at least that:

- the contractor agrees to meet obligations concerning the well-being of the workers, which are intrinsic to the establishment concerned;
- if the contractor fails to do this, or does not do so properly, the principal organisations may take any necessary steps himself.

Stage 3: Penal law obligation

Finally, the principal organisations are obliged to take any such measures, should the contractor fail to meet his obligations.

Employment agency work

Hiring workers from an external provider is a way to recruit workers. The fact that their work is temporary involves a risk that is to be managed. The Act of 24 July 1987 regarding 'temporary workers, employment agency workers and the disposing of workers to others' stipulates that the user of employment agency workers is also responsible for their health and safety. They should be protected according to the same provisions as regular workers.

Further a Central Prevention Service for the sector of employment agency work has been created by Royal Decree of 4 December 1997, in particular because of the high accident rates among temporary workers. This service is charged with the following tasks:

- organising awareness raising campaigns;
- providing training regarding the well-being at work of employment agency workers;
- collecting and disseminating material regarding the promotion of the well-being of employment agency workers;
- advising managers of employment agencies about well-being at work and the prevention of occupational risks;
- setting up studies to identify hazards and gaps in prevention measures of occupational accidents, producing and analysing statistics about occupational accidents; and carrying out studies based on qualitative and quantitative data.

OSH in public contracts

As regards government contracts, organisations must be certified to be able to take part in calls for tender procedures to obtain contracts from public organisations. The granting of government contracts in Belgium includes social as well as economic considerations. For example, companies must meet all their commitments regarding the social security of employees and deal adequately with safety and health at work. Companies who have been subject to enforcement measures by the Belgian Labour Inspectorate can be excluded form public contracts.

'Occupational safety and health is now considered as much a social matter as, for example, the interdiction of child labour or the right of free union.'

Tom De Saegher, ACW-Koepel van Christelijke Werknemersorganisaties

The issue of social clauses is the subject of debate at European level, usually for economic reasons. The European Commission is somewhat reluctant about the inclusion of social clauses. However they remain an option to be used as advocated by Belgium. These social clauses include occupational safety and health as an equally important social matter as, for example, the interdiction of child labour or the right of free union.

7.2.3. Current use of the system

The compliance rate with the procedure of the 'three green lights' is increasing. Since the introduction of CE marking, the procedure of purchasing has become complementary to the framework directive on occupational safety and health, and this approach is working well. The procedure is now meant to analyse whether the work equipment fits in its specific workplace and functions in its specific use. As such it is part of the mandatory risk assessment.

The disclosure of information about dangerous substances is an obligation that applies to all suppliers of substances which can become dangerous when used by workers. The obligation is linked to the specific use of a substance by each employer.

On a statutory basis the system applies to all cases where companies carry out activities at the same place.

The Central Prevention Service the sector of employment agency work has started in November 1998, with a central department of three OSH specialists and a liaison person in each of the 100 certified agencies.

The obligations apply to all public tenders.

7.2.4. Experiences

With respect to the purchase of work equipment and protective equipment it can mentioned that over 50 % of the large companies comply with the regulatory provisions. This is obviously less in smaller companies. Therefore External Prevention and Protection at Work Services have been created to support smaller and medium-sized companies. Experiences are positive in large as well as in smaller companies.

With respect to the purchase of dangerous substances the provisions are too recent to make an assessment of experiences. However there seems to be a move to more disclosure of information. Before, limited disclosure was only possible to occupational physicians.

In the construction sector and also in the chemical sector where the issue of working with contractors and third parties is most prominent there is a tendency to use more objective criteria to select contractors. Further there are indications that the coordination of contractors has been improved, as well as the actual control and surveillance of the contractors by the principals.

Since the establishment of the Central Service for the Sector of Employment Agency Work there has also been better coordination on safety issues

'A central service enables us to deal adequately with those professions and sectors that pose the biggest OSH problems for agency workers.'

Hendrik De Lange, director of P&I Experiences

concerning employment agency workers, especially in larger agencies. The compliance with the regulations has improved. Data are collected for the sector to provide a better knowledge on accidents, risk professions and risk sectors. Smaller and new employment agencies are more frequently seeking for direct help, information and advice.

Finally with respect to OSH in public contracts it can be mentioned that the companies certified for public tender that have been subject to a measure by Labour Inspectorate within the past five years are now invited by the certification commission to present their case regarding occupational safety and health. Sometimes temporary suspension of the certificate is ordered. About 15 cases are examined every year.

7.2.5. Impression of effectiveness and scale of application

<u>Purchase of work equipment and protective equipment</u>: The statistics from the Labour Inspectorate between 1996 and 2000 show that 56 % of the inspected companies comply with the regulations on the procurement of work and protective equipment:

Score	0	1	2	3	4
	29 %	15 %	34 %	19 %	4 %
	Non-compliance		**Compliance**		
	44 %		56 %		

0: No procedure
1: No expert advice of internal prevention adviser
2: Strict compliance (eventually minor offences)
3: OSH expert advice of other people within the company
4: OSH expert advice of other people outside the company

There are strong indications that the compliance with the regulations is increasing. Moreover, from practical experience it can be concluded that the system seems to be particularly successful in larger companies. Since the Act on well-being at work came into force companies have been obliged to hire an External Prevention and Protection at Work Service when the expertise available within the company is not adequate. These services started from 1 January 2000. An increased compliance is expected on the procurement rules in the next years.

Purchase of dangerous substances: The statistics from the Belgian Labour Inspectorate between 1996 and 2000 show that 74 % of the inspected companies comply with the regulation:

Score	0	1	2	3	4
	5 %	11 %	55 %	25 %	4 %
	Non-compliance		Compliance		
	26 %	74 %			

0: More hazardous products than needed in the workplace
1: Unidentified or bad labelled products in the workplace
2: Strict compliance (eventually minor offences)
3: Identification documents of all products available
4: Risk analysis regarding used products and implementation of measures

These figures actually reflect the implementation of the regulation regarding the current products. Identification documents in this regulation contain data about the intrinsic characteristics (e.g. chemical and physical) of the substances. They are not as such related to specific use in the actual workplace. Therefore a new Act regarding Hazardous Substances has been adopted. Effectiveness or scale of implementation of the latter is however not yet available. Presently only in 4 % of the inspected companies is a real risk assessment of the use of hazardous products carried out.

Working with contractors and third parties: Since the system has only recently been introduced, its effectiveness and scale of implementation is still difficult to assess. However the following trends can be observed.

- Non statutory certification systems such as the Dutch VCA and the Belgian Besacc are increasingly used by companies to help them comply with their obligation of precaution.
- Better work conditions have resulted and fewer violations of regulation have been observed.

Employment Agency workers: Initiatives have been taken in each field of action of the Central Service for the Employment Sector of Agency Work — i.e. awareness raising, advice, advice and research. Data about accidents occurring to agency workers have been produced. The analysis shows that on one hand, there is a positive evolution of the figures in the larger agencies. On the other hand, accidents to employment agency workers are still more serious than to regular workers. Also the collection of sector information has started, allowing limited conclusions on the frequency, seriousness and causes of work accidents, for example amongst student workers.

Campaigns to employment agency workers are better coordinated and extended: for example: distribution of safety agenda, 'student workers' action, and 'first mission' action. Awareness-raising for users of employment agency workers, schools and training institutions has become more possible (brochures, posters, audiovisual means). Further the training of the liaison people (one for each agency) has increased (basic training and regular refreshers) and the dissemination of information to employment agencies about regulations, risks, good practices, and practical work procedures is commencing.

OSH in public contracts: The issue of OSH elements in public contracts is only applied on a limited scale. On a yearly basis about 15 companies (candidate tenderers) are examined yearly by the certification commission. So far this system has had more of an ethical appeal than a real broad scale impact on companies having a tender relation with the public sector. However there are indications that the levels of occupational safety and health of the involved companies have actually increased.

7.2.6. Further information

Mr Luc Van Hamme, Ministerie van Tewerkstelling en Arbeid (Ministry for Employment and Labour), Belliardstraat 51, B-1040 Brussels. Tel. (32-2) 233 45 43; fax (32-2) 233 45 23; e-mail: luc.vanhamme@meta.fgov.be

Employment agency workers: Mr Hendrik De Lange, Preventie en Interim/Prévention et Interim, Helihavenlaan 21/1, B-1000 Brussels. Tel. (32-2) 204 56 83; fax (32-2) 204 56 89; e-mail: hdl@p-i.be; Internet: http://www.p-i.be

8. CONCLUSIONS

Occupational safety and health in marketing and procurement

8.1 MARKETING

Marketing at company level

Just as many companies have developed their own individual schemes for procurement, the same is the situation in relation to marketing of products and services. These marketing schemes reflect the needs and priorities of the customers and the market in general. As the focus on OSH performance and qualities of products and services is increasing, there is also an increasing demand for measuring, documenting and communicating these qualities in the marketing material and to assist the customers in order to use the products and services in a safe and healthy manner.

A new trend is the more holistic approach to occupational safety and health and introduction of social and ethical aspects in the evaluation of the working environment. One example of social accounting is presented in this report. The theme is quite new when applied in an OSH context, and the experiences are therefore limited. It must however be expected that this concept will gain ground in the future and increase the focus on quality of life in the working environment.

Generic marketing systems

Certification schemes and labels based on OSH criteria have become more common as marketing tools over the last decade. Among the generic marketing systems described in this report are labelling schemes for products and equipment and certification of management systems and subcontractors based on OSH criteria.

Such schemes are often developed as results of an identified need to raise safety in relation to specific products or services. In general the presented schemes for product labelling/certification seem to promote development of more OSH-friendly products and to make it easier for purchasers to compare the OSH quality of the products and services as they are evaluated against uniform criteria. The efficiency of labels is however, dependent on continuous development in evaluation criteria and to some extent also on the number of products involved in the scheme.

Certification of contractors and management systems in the service sector in relation to OSH, has become a more strong marketing tool as it is also often a demand from the client companies in the purchasing situation. These schemes therefore go hand in hand.

Governmental marketing system

One marketing scheme initiated at governmental level is described. This scheme, which aims at certifying companies with a good OSH performance, is still in the development stage. One of the goals is to attract employees and another to establish a competitive advantage on the market. It is a so-called soft economic incentive and management incentive for improving of the OSH performance beyond what is required by the legislation. An approach which has been the target for recent research and which most likely will be further developed in more European countries in the future.

A marketing scheme as this is expected to be applicable for sectors that experience problems in attracting qualified personnel and for companies offering services to public purchasers.

8.2 PROCUREMENT

Procurement at company level

Many companies and organisations have developed their own individual procurement schemes reflecting their requirement of the products, goods and services they purchase. The motivation to develop, adopt or join a specific scheme can vary among companies and sectors. In some high-risk sectors like the construction industry the obvious risks and high accident rates and thereby the related costs and risks of delays have been key drivers in the development of some of the presented schemes. The need for improvements of occupational safety and health in this particular sector is also reflected in the number of examples presented in this report. Most successful schemes will however often be adopted and adjusted to the needs in other sectors, as this has also been the case for some of the presented schemes.

The tendency over the recent years has been to focus on the training needs for workers and supervisors and to define specific requirements for the contractors' OSH performance, requirements that are thoroughly monitored and evaluated by the client company or an independent auditor. For companies involved in this study, this approach proved to be successful. In general it resulted in a decrease in accident rates, a growing safety and health awareness, better risk management, better confidence in purchased goods, reduced costs and as an extra benefit, sometimes also cultural changes with respect to OSH within the client company.

The results in terms of better performance and continued improvements of the achieved standards, especially when buying services from contractors, is to a large extent dependent on the commitment from management. Visible and daily support from management is a key driver for lasting changes in OSH culture in the workplaces.

The presented procurement schemes can in principle be applied in every sector with a large demand for contract work and an identified need for good OSH performance. When clients make demands on their contractors, there seems to be a tendency for the contractors to pass on the same requirements to their suppliers and thereby increase the positive effects throughout the supply chain.

The same approach is used in relation to procurement of products and goods. When defining requirements for specific products already in the tender phase, it is a lot easier to prevent harmful or adverse effects from the products by simply avoiding their use.

Schemes of that kind are often customer driven or even as it is shown in one of the examples developed in a corporation between customers, suppliers and trade organisations. If the scheme gains ground its influence on product development may be significant.

Generic procurement systems

The increased amount of contract work in many high-risk sectors like the petrochemical industry, have supported the development of more generic procurement schemes for contract work, which have then been widely applied throughout the whole sector. Using uniform requirements for contractor OSH training or OSH management systems allows for a third party to carry the 'certification' or initial approval of the contractors as well the continuous improvement of the scheme.

The two presented schemes have both been developed in the petrochemical industry and have not only been widely applied within this sector but are now in a phase of developing into other sectors as well. Part of the success seem to be connected with the simplicity and practicality of the schemes and the fact that the client companies have taken part in the development of the schemes and used their experience to define the criteria.

Governmental procurement initiatives

Two procurement schemes initiated by governments are described. The scheme developed in the UK takes into account that there is a wealth of practical experience in managing safety and health, which could be shared with others — neighbouring firms, suppliers, subcontractors or the wider community. This scheme is widely applicable in all sectors and provides a number of benefits to those who join the scheme — the good neighbours. These benefits include better confidence in the business partners due to increased OSH awareness, the scheme adds to the neighbours experience with contract work and enhances their reputation among business partners and in the community.

The other scheme, which originates from Belgium is based on the development of a number of procedures in the field of purchasing. These procedures cover purchasing of work equipment, protective equipment, dangerous substances, working with contractors, employment agency work and OSH in public contracts. The overall purpose is to control OSH risks in Belgium companies. Unlike the other schemes, this scheme is based on compulsory procedures, which however go beyond the requirements defined in the European directives in this area and can act as inspiration for other also voluntary schemes. The scheme can be applied in all sectors.

8.3 SCALE OF APPLICATION

This report has presented a number of examples of how different companies include OSH in their marketing and procurement procedures and how these activities add to their general business performance. These examples are meant to inspire other companies and organisations either to adopt or join the schemes or to make the necessary modifications to adapt the schemes to their specific sector and needs. Some companies might even find inspiration to develop new schemes in cooperation with others. The main issue is that occupational safety and health is an important area that is not only crucial for the workers in each individual company but can also be crucial to keep companies healthy and successful.

In many countries the social partners have become increasingly involved in voluntary schemes promoting safety and health at the workplaces. Either by supporting the schemes once they are implemented or through direct partnership and participation in running the schemes.

In Europe a lot of companies, workers and end users of marketed products and services have already been influenced by the presented schemes, which have been implemented in many different sectors. In the table below, an overview of the current use of the schemes and the possible areas where the schemes potentially could be applied in the future are presented.

Case company/example	Current use	Relevance for other product groups or sectors
Linjebus	Preparation of social accounts is in a preliminary stage in Denmark and no common standard is available. Social accounts certified against the international standard SA8000 are only issued in two European countries.	Social accounts will probably be most relevant for service companies like transport operators, welfare work, cleaning contractors and in other branches marketing services.
Fiskars	The specific combination of methods for product development which are described are primarily used in the Eurohandtool project, although elements are generally used.	The methods can most likely be applied in other areas where hand-tools or even power-driven tools are used, e.g. agriculture, construction and assembly work.
König + Neurath	The holistic marketing strategy for office furniture, is developed and used by König + Neurath alone.	A modified form of the marketing strategy seems particularly suitable for manufacturers of workplace equipment for different sectors, e.g. electrical engineering, sewing, laboratories, supermarkets and manufacturers of gardening tools and home office furniture — areas where ergonomics and other OSH-related criteria play an important role.

Case company/example	Current use	Relevance for other product groups or sectors
Polytop	The initiative is taken and used by the German supplier of car care products Polytop. The initiative includes OSH consultancy and support to the customers buying Polytop's products. Furthermore support is provided to the customers regarding implementation of employer obligations in terms of OSH.	The marketing approach can apply to chemical manufacturers, who wish to market their products as OSH friendly and will make an effort supporting their customers with OSH knowledge.
Vedior BIS	The scheme was introduced in 1994 by the French organisation Vedior BIS in order to market temporary workers, which have received specific OSH training. The OSH qualifications are a 'guarantee' for the companies employing the temporary workers. The training service is provided by more agencies organised under Vedior BIS.	The scheme can be applied to staff agencies for temporary workers, who will promote the temporary workers by improving their OSH skills.
Indoor climate label used by Rockfon	The label is available in Denmark and Norway. The label was introduced in 1995 by a private Danish organisation, representing manufacturers of building products, suppliers, trade organisations and R & D institutions. Requirements and test standards have been developed for a variety of building materials such as ceiling and wall systems, textile flooring, doors and folding partitions, resilient floorings, laminated-, and wood-based floors, oils for wooden floors, windows, kitchen, bath and wardrobe cabinets.	Private groups representing the building material sector in other countries could enter the international committee, together with the Danish and Norwegian groups, in order to apply the scheme in other countries.
TCO label	The label was introduced in 1992 by the Swedish trade union TCO. The label is used worldwide by manufactures marketing their IT equipment as OSH and environmentally sound. From 1999 the label has been available for products as displays, system units, keyboards, printers, fax and copy-machines.	The label is applicable to private or public institutions, trade unions or national authorities, who would motivate companies to develop and market OSH and environmentally sound products. Advisory similar labels should focus on other products with a larger professional application than IT equipment and products already labelled with an eco-label.
6E-TCO	The OSH and environmental management systems are introduced by the Swedish trade union TCO. The system is developed specifically for smaller companies and assists the companies in the process towards a 6E certification. Currently two Swedish companies are certified and another 23 are in process.	The scheme can be applied to private or public institutions, trade unions or national authorities, which would motivate and assist smaller companies to obtain a OSH focused certificate as a marketing tool.
NF HSA label used by Bongard	The labelling scheme is introduced by the cake and bread-making equipment manufacturer, Bongard, which market their bakery equipment using the label.	The labelling scheme can be applied to more manufacturers of bakery equipment and modified labelling schemes could be developed for other kinds of equipment.
Danish working environment label	The label/certificate is still not in use. A pilot project is initiated and will support the political decision about whether the label/certificate should be implemented or not.	Other institutions, national authorities, trade unions interested in providing companies with a OSH marketing tool.
Øresund fixed link	The described initiatives were applied during the construction of the Øresund link, which started in 1993 and was finalised in July 2000. The Danish landworks represented approximately 4.6 million working hours.	The same initiatives may be applied in relation to other large construction projects in particular, but also smaller projects could benefit form using the scheme.

Case company/example	Current use	Relevance for other product groups or sectors
Renault Technocenter	The described initiatives were applied during the construction of Renault Technocenter, which was finalised in 1998. The site represented 9 million working hours distributed between 900 contractors and 10 000 persons.	The same initiatives can be applied especially to larger construction work where many contractors are involved. The principle of involving all key players in the project in the OSH work is universal.
Electrabel	The Besacc scheme, which can be used for contractors to evaluate their own performance and for clients to assess potential contractors is widely used in Belgium.	Other industrial sectors and large companies using many contractors could apply modifications of the Besacc scheme.
AstraZeneca	The described system represents the AstraZeneca way of managing safety, health and environmental issues, and has been in use since the merger in 1999.	The managing system is applicable to all types of industries, which are dependent on stable suppliers and contract workers.
IKA	The guidelines for cleaning agents were developed in 1996 and have, up to February 2000, been used in relation to 75 tenders prepared by municipalities and 12 tenders prepared by counties.	The guidelines are particularly applicable for large companies and public institutions preparing tenders for cleaning agents. Guidelines could easily be prepared for other product groups and OSH considerations be implemented to a larger extent.
BeschaffungsService Austria	The guidelines including OSH criteria, developed in Austria for public procurement have so far been developed for product groups including cleaning agents, paints, chemicals and office furniture.	Similar guidelines can be prepared for, in principle, all product groups purchased by public institutions. In Europe public purchasing accounts for up to 20 % of the gross national product.
The Dutch VCA system	Until the year 2000 about 7 000 VCA certificates have been issued and every year 1 500 new certificates are awarded. More than 200 000 national safety passports have been issued to workers in VCA-certified companies. The scheme is used in construction, chemical, petrochemical, and metal industry.	Like the Besacc scheme, other industrial sectors and large companies using many contractors could apply modifications of the VCA scheme.
The passport training scheme	In 1999 the number of passport holders in the UK was 114 000 and the scheme was used by more than 120 individual companies. The safety passport training scheme is used in the construction, engineering, and paper industry all over UK and it is on its way in Ireland.	The passport training scheme can easily be adopted by other industrial sectors using contract workers. The plan is also to support implementation in other European countries.
Services procured through Biganos EIG (econonmic interest grouping) by Smurfit — Cellulose du Pin	The scheme was introduced by Smurfit in order to manage procurement and safety of OSH-trained contractors through an economic interest grouping. The OSH qualifications are a 'guarantee' for the company Smurfit, who employ the trained contractors. More econonmic interest groups are now using the scheme offering training and services.	The scheme can apply to other companies who to a large extent use contractors and groups of contractors offering services.
Triodos Bank	The described screening process based on ethical issues including OSH is that of Triodos Bank. Ethical investment (including OSH criteria) in general is gaining ground and in the UK the ethical investments have increased from GBP 280 million in 1990 to GBP 2 billion in 1998 and in the same period the number of funds has grown from 18 to 24.	Ethical investment can be applied to the financial sector all over Europe.

Case company/example	Current use	Relevance for other product groups or sectors
The good neighbour scheme	The good neighbour scheme applies throughout the UK. Good neighbour forums have been held in six locations, each forum involving around 120 people from different sectors.	The scheme seems to be widely applicable across all sectors and size of company due to the general relevance of the principles behind it.
Procurement policy in Belgium	The scheme applies in Belgium, where a number of OSH procedures going further than the European OSH directives have been implemented. With respect to purchasing of work equipment and protective equipment and dangerous substances the compliance rate is among 56 to 74 %.	The procurement procedures seem to be widely applicable across all sectors and size of company purchasing work equipment, protective equipment, dangerous substances and services.

European Agency for Safety and Health at Work

Appendix 1 METHODOLOGY AND DATA COLLECTION

In May 1999, the European Agency for Safety and Health at Work published a call for tender for the project 'Occupational safety and health as a subject for subcontracting and marketing'. COWI, Consulting Engineers and Planners AS from Denmark was chosen as main contractor together with four subcontractors Eurogip (France), TNO Work and Employment (Netherlands), Systemkonzept (Germany) and PPM (Austria). Prevent (Belgium) was hired as a subcontractor to Eurogip. The UK Health and Safety Executive has prepared the description of the UK good neighbour scheme, and the Belgian ministry for Employment and Labour has prepared a description on their national policy on procurement.

A project team was composed and consistent of the following persons:

Ms Sonja Hagen Mikkelsen, Project Manager	COWI
Ms Marchen Vinding Petersen	COWI
Ms Karin Rothmann Hansen	COWI
Mr Jean-Loup Wannepain	Eurogip
Ms Ellen Voullaire	Systemkonzept
Mr Alfred Brouwers	TNO
Mr Gerhard Elsigan	PPM

Aim of the project.

The aim of the project was to identify and describe a number of cases or examples about the ways:

- purchasers of products, goods and services (private enterprises and public institutions) select subcontractors/suppliers on the basis of their safety and health performances;
- suppliers of products and services market their products, goods and services (on a voluntary basis) through labels, declarations or general communications. In particular when they declare that their products/services are safe to be used in a work situation or produced under good internal working conditions.

The purpose with the catalogue is to inspire companies, sector organisations, administrations and other groups interested in new ways to improve occupational safety and health (OSH) and provide information that can help them identify for them suitable approaches.

Method applied

A number of companies promoting OSH through their procurement or marketing procedures have been selected and the case studies describing the different schemes in use are based on interviews with number of informants within companies and other relevant interest groups.

The criteria to include the companies was that their OSH-related initiatives did go beyond the minimum levels defined in the regulations or that the specific initiatives supported the practical implementation of good safety and health practices in the workplace.

The companies and schemes which are represented in the study are selected among those known to the project team or proposed by the Agency in order to have a maximum number of Member States represented in the study. A larger number of other companies and organisations were approached from the beginning and asked to take part. However, not all of these were able to participate at the given time and some schemes were left out and substituted by others during the project period, because the focus on OSH was concluded to be to weak. The final selection of schemes to be described can therefore not be considered representative to all the initiatives in place in the European Union although the project team has made an effort to make the best possible selection. In order to perform the case studies in a systematic and comparable way, three interview guides and five questionnaires directed to specific groups of key respondents were prepared.

In general the interviewed groups included:

- developers of the specific schemes used to define supplier requirements or to document marketing statements;
- companies selecting contractors or suppliers based on their OSH performance. Typically informants represented senior management, OSH expert(s) and purchaser(s) within the company. Furthermore, information was obtained from users of the procured products or services either by sending out a questionnaire or by carrying out telephone interviews. Also the suppliers of the products or services met with OSH requirements were asked in order to evaluate the impact of the scheme on product development and to point out the potential difficulties fulfilling the OSH requirements;
- companies highlighting OSH qualities related to their products or services in their marketing. Typically, informants included marketing- and sale expert(s), product developer(s) and OSH expert(s). Additionally, customers of these products or services were contacted and interviewed via telephone or asked to fill in a questionnaire about their experiences with the products or services.

Before carrying out the interviews, an information letter with a short introduction to the project, the organisation, the process and expected outcome, was sent out to the participating key respondents.

A kick-off meeting for the project team was arranged before the data collection was started. The purpose of the meeting was to discuss the methodology and the interview guides in order to ensure a common understanding and homogeneity in carrying out the interviews.

If desired the interview guides and questionnaires are available on the home page of the European Agency for Safety and Health. Internet: http://agency.osha.eu.int/report/procurement

Appendix 2 ACKNOWLEDGEMENTS

The European Agency for Safety and Health at Work would like to thank Sonja Hagen Mikkelsen and Marchen Vinding Petersen from COWI (Denmark) for this valuable report, not least because they have covered a rather new area of occupational safety and health.

On behalf of COWI we would also like to thank those organisations that provided support in describing case studies: Eurogip (France), TNO Arbeid (Netherlands), Systemkonzept (Germany) and PPM (Austria). Further we would like to thank the Health and Safety Executive (United Kingdom), and the Belgian ministry for Employment and Labour for their contributions to the report.

Furthermore we would like to thank all those companies that were willing to be subject in this study. A large number of people have kindly contributed with information, either by answering questionnaires or by participating in interviews. Many companies have opened their doors and have shared their experiences with the project team and without their contributions the project could not have been completed. In particular we would like to express our gratitude to the following organisations:

AstraZeneca, United Kingdom
BeschaffungsService, Austria
Biganos EIG, France
Bongard, France
Electrabel, Belgium
Fiskars, Finland
The Health and Safety Executive, United Kingdom
IKA, Denmark
König + Neurath, Germany
Linjebus, Denmark
Ministry for Employment and Labour, Belgium
Nokia, Sweden
Polytop, Germany
Renault Technocenter, France
Rockfon, Denmark
Smurfit — Cellulose du Pin, France
Texaco, United Kingdom
TCO, Sweden
VCA, Netherlands
National Working Environment Authority, Denmark
Representatives from Øresundskonsortiet, Denmark

Finally the agency would like to thank the members of the Thematic Network Group Systems and Programmes for their comments and suggestions with respect to the planning of this project as well as for their comments on earlier versions of this report.

Martin den Held

Project Manager, Systems and Programmes

European Agency for Safety and Health at Work

Occupational safety and health in marketing and procurement

Luxembourg: Office for Official Publications of the European Communities

2000 — 172 pp. — 16,2 x 22,9 cm

ISBN 92-95007-01-8

Price (excluding VAT) in Luxembourg: EUR 9